Knowledge Management for Teams and Projects

CHANDOS
KNOWLEDGE MANAGEMENT SERIES

Series Editor: Melinda Taylor
(email: melindataylor@chandospublishing.com)

Chandos' new series of books are aimed at all those individuals interested in knowledge management. They have been specially commissioned to provide the reader with an authoritative view of current thinking. If you would like a full listing of current and forthcoming titles, please visit our web site **www.chandospublishing.com** or contact Hannah Grace-Williams on email info@chandospublishing.com or telephone number +44 (0) 1865 884447.

New authors: we are always pleased to receive ideas for new titles; if you would like to write a book for Chandos, please contact Dr Glyn Jones on email gjones@chandospublishing.com or telephone number +44 (0) 1865 884447.

Bulk orders: some organisations buy a number of copies of our books. If you are interested in doing this, we would be pleased to discuss a discount. Please contact Hannah Grace-Williams on email info@chandospublishing.com or telephone number +44 (0) 1865 884447.

Knowledge Management for Teams and Projects

NICK MILTON

Chandos Publishing
Oxford · England

Chandos Publishing (Oxford) Limited
Chandos House
5 & 6 Steadys Lane
Stanton Harcourt
Oxford OX29 5RL
UK
Tel: +44 (0) 1865 884447 Fax: +44 (0) 1865 884448
Email: info@chandospublishing.com
www.chandospublishing.com

First published in Great Britain in 2005

ISBN:
1 84334 114 X (paperback)
1 84334 115 8 (hardback)

© N. Milton, 2005

British Library Cataloguing-in-Publication Data.
A catalogue record for this book is available from the British Library.

Typeset at Domex e-Data Pvt. Ltd.
Printed in the UK and USA.

Contents

List of figures

List of tables

About the author

Dr Nick Milton has been working in the field of knowledge management since 1992. He is a director and co-founder of Knoco Ltd – a knowledge management consultancy providing knowledge management services to a range of national and multinational clients in the oil and gas, mining, consumer goods, engineering, education and other sectors. Nick acts as KM consultant and trainer for drilling projects within British Petroleum (BP), and has recently been involved in a review of knowledge management within BP's major capital projects. During the early 2000s he was involved with implementing KM in projects within De Beers. Nick's areas of current focus are:

- knowledge management assessment, strategy and implementation planning;
- project-specific knowledge management plans;
- knowledge capture, packaging and re-use.

Prior to founding Knoco Ltd, Nick acted as Knowledge Manager for the BP Knowledge Management Team. This team spent two years developing and implementing a process by which the business could make maximum benefit of the knowledge and experience within the organisation. They delivered $260m in measurable benefit to BP business units through 1998 pilot projects alone. Nick's role in this team was to build and perfect the KM methods and approach, and to act as a coach and trainer for people in the business. His specific achievements were:

- developing a practical system for knowledge management;
- engaging business units world wide in the value of KM;
- building and sustaining a KM 'community of practice';
- acting as global consultant and advisor for KM activities;
- developing and delivering events for training business staff in the implementation of KM for business benefit;

- organising, collating, packaging and deploying BP's knowledge assets for key business topics;
- facilitating major knowledge-capture and exchange events.

Nick also spent five years as Quality Advisor and Knowledge Manager for BP Norway, during that business' most successful period for over a decade. His background and training are in the field of petroleum exploration geology.

Nick has an MA in Natural Sciences (1st Class) from the University of Cambridge, UK, and a PhD from the University of Wales. He lives in Bath, UK with his son.

The author may be contacted at:

E-mail: *nick.milton@knoco.co.uk*
Tel: +44 (0)7803 592947

Principles of knowledge management

Introduction

It is traditional to start a book of this type with the discussion of 'what is knowledge', and 'what is knowledge management'. If you are already quite clear about the distinction, then this chapter is not for you. However, there is often still some confusion over the definitions of, and fuzzy boundaries between, knowledge management, information management and data management. The two latter disciplines are well established; people know what they mean, people are trained in them, there are plenty of reference books to explain what they are and how they work. *Knowledge management*, on the other hand, is a relatively new term, and one that requires a little bit of explanation. If you would rather jump on to the practical applications, then start at Chapter 2, and come back to Chapter 1 another day.

We will start by looking at 'what is knowledge'.

What is knowledge?

Knowledge is something which only humans can possess. People know things, computers can't know things. Traditionally, in our schooling system and in many organisations, knowledge is seen as a personal possession. If you are a knowledgeable person, you have status and you are in demand. Knowledge gives you the ability to take action. Knowledge is based on experience, it requires information, and it involves the application of theory or heuristics[1] (either consciously or unconsciously), and it allows you to make knowledgeable decisions. Knowledge has something which data and information lack, and those extra ingredients are the experience and the heuristics.

As an illustration, consider the link between data, information and knowledge as they are involved in decision making in a mining exploration company.

The company pays for a mineralogy survey, taking samples across an area of mountainous country. Each sample is analysed, and each analysis is a datapoint. These data are held in a database.

In order for these data to be interpreted, they need to be presented in a meaningful way. The company uses a geographical information system to present the data in map form. A contour map of the mineralogical data represents information, showing the pattern of changes in the mineralogy across the mountain belt.

However, this map needs to be interpreted. Such information, even presented in map form, is meaningless to the layman, but an experienced mining geologist can look at it, apply their experience, use some theory, heuristics or rules of thumb, and can make a decision. That decision may be to conduct some further sampling, to open a mine, or to dismiss the area as unprospective.

The mining geologist has 'know-how' – he or she knows how to interpret contour maps of mineralogical data. They can use that knowledge to take information (presented in the map), and decide which action to take. That know-how is developed from training, from years of experience, through the acquisition of a set of heuristics and working models, and through many conference and bar-room conversations with the wider community of mining geologists (see Figure 1.1).

Knowledge which leads to action is 'know-how'. Your experience, and the theories and heuristics to which you have access, allow you to know

Figure 1.1   The data – information – knowledge – action link

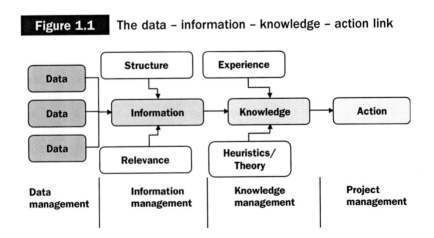

what to do, and to know how to do it. In this book, you can use the terms 'knowledge' and 'know-how' interchangeably.

In large organisations, and in organisations where people work in teams and networks, knowledge and know-how are increasingly being seen as a communal possession, rather than an individual possession. Communities of practice (see Chapter 4) are networks of people who have collective ownership of knowledge. Such knowledge is 'common knowledge' – the things that 'everybody knows'. This common knowledge is based on shared experiences, and on collective theory and heuristics that are defined, agreed and validated by the community.

Shared experience is often hard to codify, and is transferred within a project by communication and learning meetings, and between projects by processes such as peer assists, technical limit, optioneering, and action learning (all of which are described in this book). The theories and heuristics can be written down and codified into case histories, lessons learned, project best practices, and (ultimately) company policies and standards. This codification process will be described later.

Tacit and explicit knowledge

The terms *tacit* and *explicit* are often used when talking about knowledge. The original authors, Nonaka and Takeuchi (1995) use these terms to define 'unable to be expressed' and 'able to be expressed' respectively. Thus, in the original usage, tacit knowledge means knowledge held instinctively, in the unconscious mind and in the muscle memory, which cannot be transferred in words alone. Knowledge of how to ride a bicycle, for example, is tacit knowledge, as it is almost impossible to explain verbally.

Nowadays these original definitions have become blurred, and tacit and explicit are often used to describe 'knowledge which has not been codified' and 'knowledge which has been codified' (or 'head knowledge' and 'recorded knowledge' respectively). This latter definition is a more useful one in the context of knowledge management within projects, as it defines knowledge based on where it exists, rather than on its intrinsic codifiability. So, knowledge which exists only in people's heads is termed *tacit knowledge*, and knowledge which has been recorded somewhere is termed *explicit knowledge*. Tacit knowledge can therefore be made explicit if is captured and recorded.

There is a wide range of types of knowledge, from easily codifiable to completely uncodifiable. Some know-how, such as how to cook a pizza, can be codified and written down; indeed, most households contain

Figure 1.2 The varying codifiability of knowledge: some tasks (such as cooking, or constructing a garden shed) are relatively simple and easily codifiable. Others may be quite simple (riding a bike), but very hard to codify

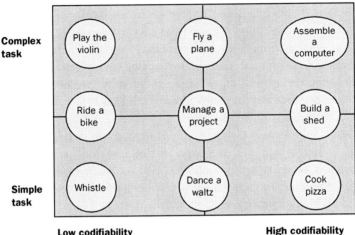

codified cooking knowledge (cookery books). Other know-how, such as how to ride a bicycle, cannot be codified, and there would be no point in trying to teach someone to ride a bike by giving them a book on the subject.

Project knowledge sits in the middle of the graph in Figure 1.2. Some of it can be codified, some can't. Some can be captured and made explicit, some can't. This assertion has implications for how project knowledge will be managed, because it means we need to address both the tacit and explicit dimensions.

What is knowledge management?

If knowledge is a combination of experience, theory and heuristics, developed by an individual or a community of practice, which allows decisions to be made and correct actions to be taken, then what is knowledge management? Larry Prusak, of McKinsey Consulting, says 'It is the attempt to recognise what is essentially a human asset buried in the minds of individuals, and leverage it into a corporate asset that can be used by a broader set of individuals, on whose decisions the firm depends'. Larry is here suggesting that the shift from seeing knowledge as personal property, to seeing knowledge as communal property, is at the heart of knowledge management. To ensure management discipline, we need to make sure that the leverage to which Larry refers is done systematically, routinely and in service of business strategy.

Gorelick et al. (2004) suggest that 'knowledge management is fundamentally a systematic approach for optimising the access, for individuals and teams within an organisation, to relevant actionable advice, knowledge and experience from elsewhere'. This definition is similar to that of Prusak, although it looks at knowledge from the point of view of the knowledge user rather than the knowledge supplier. It also emphasises the need for the knowledge to be relevant and actionable, and therefore valuable to the knowledge user.

If you read widely about knowledge management, or attend many of the conferences, you will discover that for many people, 'knowledge management' is currently not a popular term. Some people challenge whether knowledge could ever be managed. They point to the intangible tacit nature of knowledge, the difficulty of separating knowledge from people, the difficulty of measuring the flow of knowledge, and suggest that this makes knowledge effectively unmanageable. Terms like 'knowledge sharing', 'systematic learning', 'shared learning' are often proposed instead.

However, modern businesses are becoming increasingly familiar with the practice of managing intangibles. Risk management, customer relations management, safety management, and brand management are all recognised management approaches. Knowledge is not significantly less tangible or measurable than risk, brand, or safety, and the term 'management' suggests a healthy level of rigour and business focus. The value of a brand is enormous, and therefore brands need to be managed. The value of corporate knowledge is also enormous, so why should that value not also be managed? Brand, reputation, knowledge, customer base etc, are intangible assets with great value to the organisation, and to leave these assets unmanaged would seem to be foolish in the extreme.

The terminology you use, however, is less important than the approach you take. If people don't like the term 'knowledge management', then you can avoid using the term initially. However, there is no need to be apologetic about applying the term 'management' to knowledge, and the term 'knowledge management' is a useful reminder, when knowledge sharing has proven its value, that knowledge needs to be captured, shared and applied with a degree of managed rigour.

Knowledge management models

In this section we will look at some simple models for the management of knowledge, and develop a 12-component model that looks at the stock and flow of knowledge, and some of the enabling factors that need to be in place to enable the flow and replenish the stock. Some of the ideas and models introduced here will be built upon through the rest of the book.

Knowledge suppliers and users

The definitions presented in the previous section imply the existence of suppliers of knowledge, and users of knowledge; people in whose minds the knowledge is buried, and people and teams who need access to that knowledge.

Knowledge is created through experience, and through the reflection on experience in order to derive guidelines, rules, theories, heuristics and doctrines. Knowledge may be created by individuals, through reflecting on their own experience, or it may be created by teams reflecting on team experience. It may also be created by experts or communities of practice reflecting on the experience of many individuals and teams across an organisation. The individuals, teams and communities who do this reflecting can be considered as 'knowledge suppliers'.

In business activity, knowledge is applied by individuals and teams. They can apply their own personal knowledge and experience, or they can look elsewhere for knowledge – to learn before they start. The more knowledgeable they are at the start of the activity or project, the more likely they are to avoid mistakes, repeat good practice, and avoid risk. These people are 'knowledge users'.

We have introduced the idea of tacit knowledge and explicit knowledge. The knowledge can be transferred from the supplier to the user tacitly, through dialogue, or explicitly, through codifying the knowledge. Figure 1.3 shows these two approaches, by looking at the two places where knowledge can be stored: in people's heads, or in codified form in some sort of 'knowledge bank'. These two stores can be connected in four ways:

- direct transfer of knowledge from person to person (communication);
- transfer of knowledge from people to the 'knowledge bank' (knowledge capture, making tacit knowledge explicit);

Figure 1.3 The flow of knowledge from supplier to user

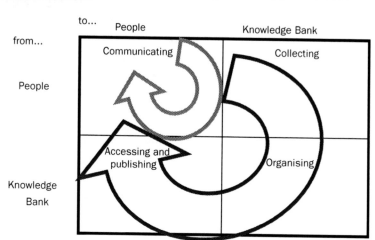

- organisation of knowledge within the knowledge bank (organisation);
- transfer of knowledge from the 'knowledge bank' back to people (access and retrieval).

Knowledge can therefore flow from supplier to user (from person to person, or team to team) in two ways.

The most direct (the upper left arrow on Figure 1.3) is through direct communication and dialogue. Face-to-face dialogue, or e-mail discussion, is an extremely effective means of knowledge transfer. This method allows vast amounts of detailed knowledge to be transferred, and the context for that knowledge to be explored. It allows direct coaching, observation and demonstration. However, it is very localised. The transfer takes place in one place at one time, involving only the people in the conversation.[2] For all its effectiveness as a transfer method, it is not efficient. For direct communication and dialogue to be the only knowledge transfer mechanism within an organisation, would require a high level of travel and discussion, and may only be practical in a small company working out of a single office where travel is not an issue. This may be the only practical approach to the transfer of uncodifable knowledge (teaching someone to ride a bicycle can only be done face to face). However, it should not be the only mechanism of knowledge transfer, nor should knowledge be stored only as tacit knowledge in people's heads. Using people's memories as the primary place for storing knowledge is a very risky strategy. Memories are unreliable, people forget, misremember, or post-rationalise. People leave the company, retire, or join the competition. For example, what is the staff turnover in your team? Your division? Your company? How much knowledge is leaving your organisation in the heads of the departing people? There needs to be a more secure storage mechanism for crucial knowledge, and a more efficient means of transfer than just dialogue.

The less direct flow of knowledge (the larger, lower right arrow on Figure 1.3) is through codification and capture of the knowledge, storage in some sort of 'knowledge bank', and retrieval of the knowledge when needed. The transfer is lower bandwidth than direct communication, as it is difficult to write down more than a fragment of what you know. No dialogue is possible, and demonstrations are restricted to video files. Transfer of knowledge by this means is not very effective. However, the knowledge can be captured once, and accessed hundreds of times, so it is an efficient method of transferring knowledge widely. The knowledge is secure against memory loss, or loss of personnel. This approach is ideal for codifiable knowledge with a wide user base. For example, the widespread transfer of cooking knowledge is best done through publishing cookery books. It is also ideal for knowledge that is used intermittently, such as knowledge of office moves, or knowledge of major acquisitions. These events may not happen again for a few years, by which time the individuals involved will have forgotten the details of what happened, if it is not captured and stored.

These two approaches to knowledge transfer are sometimes called the *connect* approach (the smaller arrow), where knowledge is transferred by connecting people, and the *collect* approach (the larger arrow), where knowledge is transferred by collecting, storing, organising and retrieving it. Each method has advantages and disadvantages, as summarised in Table 1.1. Effective knowledge management strategies need to address both these methods of knowledge transfer. Each has its place, each complements the other.

People, process, technology and culture

Systems for managing anything need to address the triple aspects of people, process and technology (see Figure 1.4). Each of these is a key enabler for any management system.

Table 1.1   The Connect and Collect approaches to Knowledge transfer

Approach	Connect	Collect
Advantages	Very effective Allows transfer of non-codifiable knowledge Allows socialisation Allows the kinowledge user to gauge how much they trust the supplier Easy and cheap	Allow systematic capture Creates a secure store for knowledge Very efficient: Knowledge can be captured once and accessed many times
Disadvantages	Risky: Human memory is an unreliable knowledge store Inefficient: People can only be in one place at one time People often don't realise what they know until its captured	Some knowledge cannot be effectively captured and codified Capturing requires skill and resource Captured knowledge can become impersonal
Types of knowledge suitable for this form of transfer	Ephemeral rapidly changing knowledge, which would be out of date as soon as its written Knowledge of continual operations, where there is a large constant community Knowledge needed only by a few	Stable mature knowledge Knowledge of intermittent or rare events High-value knowledge Knowledge with a large user-base
Comments	One traditional approach to knowledge management is to leave knowledge in the heads of experts and to transfer knowledge only through discussion: this is a risky and inefficient strategy	A strategy based only on capture will miss out on the socialisation that is needed for culture change, and may fail to address some of the less codifiable knowledge

For example, a financial management system requires people (accountants, financial managers, commercial managers), processes (budgeting, accounting, financial auditing), and technology (SAP, Sage, Quicken, spreadsheets, calculators).

Similarly, a knowledge management system needs people to be assigned roles and responsibilities; processes for knowledge identification, capture, access and sharing; and technology for the storage, organisation and retrieval of knowledge.

Figure 1.4   Enabling factors for knowledge management

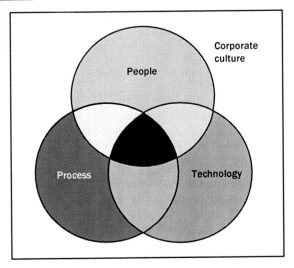

These systems of people, processes and technology will operate within a corporate culture, which needs to support the system. Financial management systems will work in a culture where money is seen to be important, where money is treated as company property rather than the property of the team or project, where wasting money is seen as a bad thing, and where a project is not seen as being properly managed unless financial management is up to standard. Similarly, knowledge management systems will work in a culture where knowledge is seen to be important, where knowledge is treated as company property rather than the property of the team or project, where wasting knowledge is seen as a bad thing, and where a project is not seen as being properly managed unless knowledge management is up to standard. See the final section of this chapter for more discussion of the cultural issues.

Knoco Ltd 12-box framework

The models presented in the previous two sections can be combined into a 12-component framework for a knowledge management system. The three enablers of people, process and technology (Figure 1.4) operate within each of the four boxes of knowledge flow (Figure 1.3) as shown in Figure 1.5.

This combination gives a 12-component framework for a knowledge management system, including:

1. people and communities with a role for communicating knowledge through discussion and dialogue;
2. structured processes of knowledge exchange through dialogue;
3. communication technologies;
4. people with a role and skills for knowledge capture;
5. processes for knowledge capture;
6. technology for capturing knowledge;
7. people with a role and skills for distilling, packaging and organising captured knowledge;
8. processes for distilling, validating, packaging etc;
9. technology for storing and presenting organised knowledge;
10. people with a role for finding knowledge or publishing new knowledge;
11. processes to ensure new knowledge is sought and published;
12. technologies for finding explicit knowledge.

If all of these 12 components are present in a knowledge management system, then the system is complete and covers all components necessary for knowledge transfer. If any of the components are missing (e.g. nobody accountable for collecting knowledge, no process for retrieval, no technology for storage), then the system will not work properly, and

Figure 1.5   Knoco Ltd 12-component framework for a knowledge management system

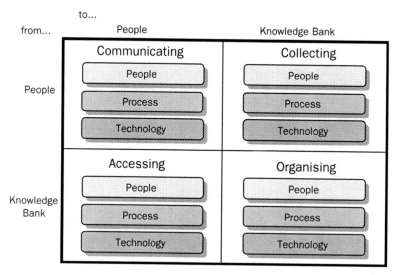

the flow of knowledge will be interrupted. We have been using this copyrighted 12-component framework in Knoco Ltd for several years now, and it has proven to be a robust and comprehensive framework. We will refer to this framework later in this book, when discussing the effectiveness of knowledge transfer systems (Chapter 5).

The 'learning before, during and after' model

The models presented in Figures 1.3–1.5 address the flow of knowledge from supplier to user, and the components that need to be in place to allow this to happen. Figure 1.6 introduces one further model, which describes how knowledge management activities can fit within the cycle of business activity.

The management of knowledge, like the management of anything else, needs to be systematic rather than ad hoc, and needs to be tied into the business cycle. In any project-focused business, where business activities (projects) have a beginning and an end, knowledge can be addressed at three points. You can learn at the start of the project, so that the project begins from a state of complete knowledge ('learning before'). You can

Figure 1.6   The learning before, during and after model

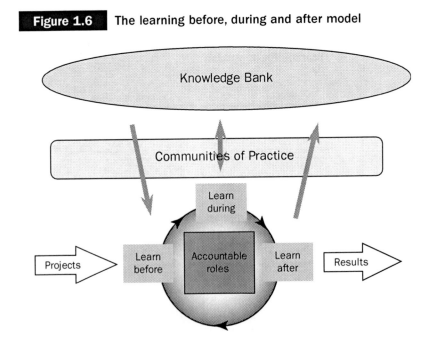

learn during the project, so that plans can be changed and adapted as new knowledge becomes available ('learning during'). Finally, you can learn at the end of the project, so that knowledge is captured for future use ('learning after'). The people and teams who manage the projects can use knowledge to improve their results and reach their goals. This model of 'learn before, during and after' was developed in BP during the 1990s, and I remember drawing the first embryonic version of the model in Shepperton, UK, in 1997. The 'learn before, during and after' model also appears to have been developed independently in several other organisations.

However, there is more to the model than just the 'learn before, during and after' cycle. The explicit knowledge generated from the project needs to be stored somewhere, in some sort of knowledge bank. Knowledge can be deposited in the bank at the end of the project, and accessed from the bank at the start of the next project. Knowledge packaged and stored in the knowledge bank can be considered to be knowledge assets.

The final components of the framework are the people components. Communities of practice need to be established to create and manage the knowledge assets and to own the tacit knowledge. Knowledge roles need to be created in the projects, to make sure that knowledge management is embedded in the business activity. Without knowledge roles, knowledge management becomes 'everyone's job', and very quickly reverts to being nobody's job.[3]

This six-component model (learning before, learning during, learning after, building knowledge assets, building communities of practice, and establishing business roles) is a robust model which creates value wherever it is applied.

Types of knowledge transfer

There is no one-size-fits-all solution for knowledge transfer, because not every transfer context is the same. One of the prime differentiators between knowledge transfer types is the relationship between the project that supplies the knowledge, and the project that needs the knowledge. Figure 1.7 shows three types of relationship.

This figure plots projects as bars of activity in time and space (location). So, for example, the three black projects are overlapping in time, but taking place in different locations. The three cross-hatched projects are in the same location, but occurring in sequence. The three grey projects are all in different places, with no overlap in time.

Figure 1.7 Three types of knowledge transfer

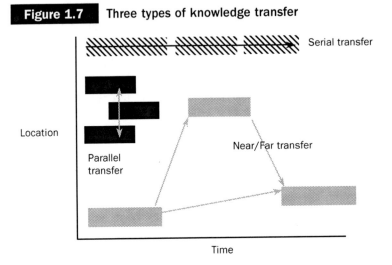

- The transfer of knowledge within a series of projects in the same location (and therefore probably with the same team) is called *serial transfer*. Much serial transfer can be accomplished by the transfer of project plans, designs, basis of design documents, and so on, as well as by transferring lessons, and transferring core team members.

- The transfer of knowledge between a series of projects running simultaneously but in different locations is called *parallel transfer*. This can rely heavily on face-to-face activities such as *peer assist*, and *knowledge visits*, as well as real-time transfer of knowledge through communities of practice and online forums. Because operations are continuous, much knowledge can remain tacit.

- The transfer of knowledge between projects running in different times and different places is called *near transfer* or *far transfer*, depending on whether the knowledge will be applied in a very similar context (near transfer), or in a different context (far transfer). Near and far transfer cannot rely on real-time conversations, or on simply transferring project plans, as the next project may take place in a completely different country in several years time. Knowledge will need to be transferred in a written form as a knowledge asset. *Near and far transfer* are terms coined by Nancy Dixon (2000), and are discussed in much more detail in Chapter 4.

It is very helpful to assess the types of knowledge transfer you need, before putting in place a knowledge management programme.

The business need for knowledge management

This section looks at the business justification for knowledge management, and where some of the value may lie. It also addresses the identification of the crucial knowledge that needs to be managed,[4] and looks at the lifecycle of knowledge within an organisation.

Business justification is crucial. If you can't clearly articulate the need for knowledge management you should not be doing it, because then you will be unclear about why you're doing it. You shouldn't be doing knowledge management because you think it's a cool, good or fashionable thing to do. You should be able to clearly outline the business reason for doing it. This section outlines two business reasons for managing knowledge: reducing the learning curve, and bringing everybody up to the benchmark.

Knowledge and performance

There is an old saying – 'It's easy when you know how'.

Any task is easy to perform, if you have the know-how. Knowledge management consists of making sure that the teams and individuals have the know-how they need, to make their task easier and to improve their performance. Knowledge feeds performance, and knowledge is also derived from performance. If your performance on a task or project is better than it was the previous time, then you have learned something. Your know-how has increased, and that know-how should be identified, analysed, codified (if possible) and disseminated to other teams. The higher your level of knowledge, the higher your level of performance. You learn from performance, and you perform by applying the knowledge you have learned. (The word 'you' in this paragraph can be singular, referring to an individual, or plural, referring to a project team or community of practice). Performance and learning can form a closed loop.

The knowledge/performance loop shown in Figure 1.8 shows the close link between these two elements, and it is fairly obvious from this link that knowledge management and performance management are also strongly linked. Knowledge management is far easier to apply in an organisation with good consistent performance metrics, a performance culture, performance measurement, reporting and target setting, and internal benchmarking. In an organisation like this, the effects of

Figure 1.8   The knowledge/performance loop

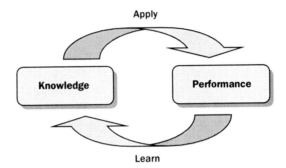

increased knowledge will be obvious, and the suppliers of knowledge (the higher performers) can be identified, as well as the customers for that knowledge (the lower performers).

Where performance is less easy to measure, knowledge management can still be applied, but it will be more difficult to make it systematic and embedded in the business process, and it will be considerably more difficult to measure the benefits.

Your knowledge management system and your performance management system should be aligned; they should operate on the same scale and to the same frequency. Generally, the periodicity of target setting and performance measuring should match the periodicity of learning and review. If targets are set for processes that take a few hours to a day (as in the technical limit process described in Chapter 3), then learning should be reviewed on a daily basis. If targets are set on a monthly basis, then they should be reviewed, and learning collected, on a monthly basis.

The learning curve

The concept of the learning curve is well-established. The longer you do something, and the more times you repeat something, the better you get. A team that works together on a series of projects will find that over time, they get better, the budgets come down, and the durations of the projects decrease. This is shown in diagrammatic form in Figure 1.9(a).

Figure 1.9(a) represents a project team which runs a programme of six projects. Over time they get better at these types of projects, and the costs (perhaps in terms of man-hours spent) come down. By the time

Figure 1.9 Knowledge management and the learning curve

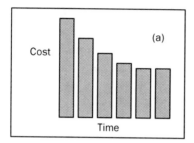

(a)

Cost

Time

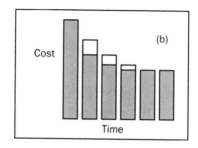

(b)

Cost

Time

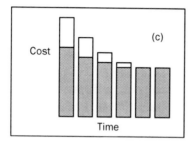

(c)

Cost

Time

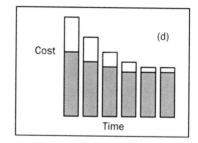

(d)

Cost

Time

they get to the fifth and sixth project, they have reached their minimum cost, and are working at their maximum efficiency. The only thing that they have at the end of this curve, which they did not have at the beginning, is knowledge. They have gained know-how, experience, guidelines and heuristics for running this sort of project.

If they manage their knowledge by concentrating on 'learning during' the programme, and transferring the knowledge from one project to the next, they may be able to learn faster. This is shown diagrammatically as shown in the solid bars in Figure 1.9(b). Here the overall cost of the programme of six projects has been reduced (by 8 per cent) by steepening the learning curve.

If they also 'learn before' the programme, by bringing in knowledge and experience from similar previous programmes, then they don't have to start at the top of the learning curve. Figure 1.9(c) shows a 16 per cent reduction for the overall cost of the six projects, by learning before the first project, and learning through the project sequence. What often happens, however, is that this focus on learning will also drive innovation, and improvements in maximum efficiency may result. The teams may exceed the maximum performance they otherwise would have achieved, as shown in Figure 1.9(d), where overall cost savings of 24 per cent have been achieved.

In BP drilling programmes, statistics suggest that the application of knowledge during a programme of multiple drilling projects, as in Figure 1.9(b), results in measurable steepening of the learning curve, and average cost savings of 7 per cent over the programme.

Benchmarking

Another way to look at the value of knowledge management, is to look at the transfer of best practices from one part of the business to another, as shown in Figure 1.10.

If you can measure and compare the performance of different teams in business units, you can identify the better performers and the poorer performance. For example, Figure 1.10(a) shows the cost performance for six different teams. High costs equate to poor performance.

Teams E and F are the best performers, operating at benchmark costs, and A and D are the worst. If all of these teams exchange knowledge, and the poorer performers learn from the better performers, then the overall performance should improve, as shown in Figure 1.10(b). All the teams except E have improved, and B and F have set a new benchmark. Considerable costs have been cut out of the system.

What frequently happens is that the better performers find that even they have things to learn, and the collective benchmark performance often improves. The cost improvement shown in Figure 1.10(b), over all six teams, is 22 per cent.

Internal benchmarking can therefore be a powerful means of measuring the value of knowledge management, and of identifying the

Figure 1.10 Knowledge management and performance benchmarking

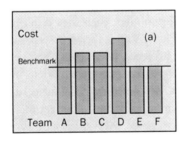
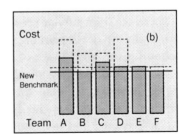

knowledge suppliers and the knowledge users (in Figure 1.10(b), teams E and F are primarily knowledge suppliers, and teams A through D are knowledge users, although to an extent all teams both supply and use knowledge).

Which knowledge?

The models shown in the previous two sections describe where the business value of knowledge lies, but not all knowledge is of equal value. Some knowledge will be crucial to your business, and some will be largely irrelevant. Some knowledge drives your core competencies, while some can be conveniently outsourced. One key component of setting your knowledge management strategy within a business, or your knowledge management plan for a project, is to define *which knowledge* – which knowledge is needed, which knowledge needs to be acquired, which knowledge will be generated, which knowledge needs to be captured and codified etc (see Chapter 5 for a discussion of knowledge management plans which define 'which knowledge' at project level).

Figure 1.11 shows a framework for deciding which knowledge to address, and how to manage it. You can start to divide knowledge topics into four areas if you look at two components: the level of in-house knowledge that currently exists, and the level of in-house need for that knowledge.

Where there is a high business need for the knowledge topic, but the level of in-house knowledge is not yet very high, then you are at the top of the learning curve, and your focus should be on rapid learning.

Where there is a high business need for the knowledge, and the level of in-house knowledge is high, then you are looking at areas of core competence, and your focus should be on development and implementation of best practice and standards.

Where there is a low business need for the knowledge, and the level of in-house knowledge is high, then you are looking at areas of old knowledge, and your focus should be on archiving this knowledge in case it is needed again in future.

Where there is a low business need for the knowledge, and the level of in-house knowledge is also low, then you might consider that this is an area of no interest in terms of knowledge management. However, it is often from this area that the new innovations arise, and areas of new technology are generated, which need to be pushed up into the 'learn rapidly' box.

Figure 1.11 Categorisation of types of knowledge. The horizontal axis measures the level of in-house knowledge – i.e. how much do you already know about this topic? The vertical axis measures how important the knowledge is to your business – i.e. how much do you need to know?

High value knowledge for your company	New knowledge – need to learn fast	Core competence – need to establish best practice
Lower value knowledge	The area where innovations come from	Old competence – need to archive
	Knowledge your company doesn't possess much of	Knowledge your company knows a lot about

An early step in development of the business knowledge management strategy, or a project knowledge management plan, is to identify the key knowledge areas and plot them on a matrix such as Figure 1.11.

Approaches to knowledge management

The more widely you read around the topic of knowledge management, the more knowledge managers you meet, and the more conferences you attend, the more you will come to realise that there are many approaches to managing knowledge. This section introduces some of these approaches, and makes the case for a holistic and systematic approach as described above.

The default approach

The default approach which many companies use, is to keep knowledge in people's heads, and to manage the knowledge by managing the people. Knowledge is owned by the experts and the experienced people. Knowledge is imported to projects by assigning experienced people as members of the project team. Knowledge is transferred from site to site by transferring staff, and by using company experts who fly around the world from project to project, identifying and spreading good practices.

This is a very traditional model, but it has many major failings, and cannot be considered to be knowledge management. Imagine if you managed your finances in this way! Imagine if the only way to fund a project was to transfer a rich person onto the project team, or to fly individual millionaires around the world to inject funds into the projects they liked!

The major drawbacks of this default 'knowledge in the heads' approach are as follows:

- Experienced people can only be on one project at a time, whereas knowledge management could spread that experience to many projects.

- Knowledge cannot be transferred until people are available for transfer.

- Experts who fly in and fly out often do not gain a good appreciation of how things are done, and where the good practices lie. In particular, teams in projects may hide their failings from the company experts, in order to be seen in a good light.

- The burn-out potential for the experts is very high.

- Knowledge can become almost 'fossilised' in the heads of the experts, who can end up applying the solutions of yesterday to the problems of today.

- When the expert leaves, retires, has a heart attack, or is recruited by the competition, the knowledge goes with them.

Unfortunately, for the experts and the experienced people, this can be an attractive model, and was stereotypical behaviour for specialist engineers for many years. It can be very exciting travelling the world, with everyone wanting your assistance. It is like early Hollywood movie scenes with the US Cavalry riding over the horizon to save the wagon train at the last minute. Knowledge management, however, would make sure that the wagon train did not get into trouble in the first place. As one experienced engineer said recently, 'If you could fly off to Russia and be a hero, or sit behind your desk and capture knowledge, what would you do?'

Partial approaches

There are many partial approaches to knowledge management, where some components of the model are applied, and others omitted. These sometimes have partial success, but nothing like the success that might be delivered by a more consistent, systematic and holistic solution. Some of the common partial solutions are listed below.

- *A technology-led approach.* Here an organisation commonly builds or buys a 'lessons learned database' where lessons can be stored, searched, and shared with other teams. Such technology can be a key component of a holistic solution, and addresses the technology components of the capture, organise and retrieve boxes of Figure 1.5. However, unless you address the people and process technologies as well, the database will either remain empty, be sporadically filled only from selected projects, or will fail to address the aspects of systematic re-use. Many organisations fall into the trap of applying a technology-led approach (possibly because it is relatively easy to buy and install a piece of technology), but find that the technology is unused. Technology is rarely the single barrier to knowledge management, and implementing technology alone is rarely sufficient. If technology were the barrier, you would see people in the organisation struggling to exchange knowledge with substandard technology such as telephones, Word documents, and paper files. It is much more common to find the barrier is lack of culture, lack of process, or lack of accountabilities.

- *A community-led approach.* A common partial approach is to implement communities of practice (see Chapter 4) as the primary knowledge management solution. Knowledge is transferred primarily in the tacit realm, along the short *connect* arrow in Figure 1.3. Sometimes the communities also take ownership of explicit knowledge, so the longer *collect* arrow is also addressed, and if this happens, then you certainly are developing a more complete knowledge management solution. However, unless the business teams and business projects are also involved in knowledge management, the 'learn before during and after' cycle in Figure 1.6 never gets deployed, and knowledge management therefore becomes decoupled from the cycles of business activity. Many companies introduce communities of practice as the 'silver bullet' – the only thing they need to manage knowledge – while in fact communities are only one dimension of a multi-dimensional solution.

- *A document-led approach.* Here an organisation introduces document management as its approach to knowledge management. It assumes that the majority of knowledge is held in explicit form in documents, and feels that if these documents can be organised, stored, searched and retrieved (perhaps using techniques such as data mining, text summarisation and natural-language searching), then knowledge will be shared. Unfortunately, this is an extremely ineffective way of managing knowledge. Many documents contain far more data and information than knowledge, and unless there is a systematic owned process for knowledge identification and capture, then most of the knowledge will never make it into document form in the first place. In addition, unless there is a systematic owned process for knowledge validation, distillation and organisation, then knowledge will become diluted and irretrievable in a sea of irrelevant documentation. Finally, this approach deals with only explicit knowledge, and will not address those components of knowledge that have to remain tacit because they are uncodifiable.

The holistic approach

The approach to knowledge management advocated in this book is a holistic approach, which addresses all of the dimensions. The models shown in Figures 1.3–1.6 are combined into a system that addresses:

- tacit knowledge (in people's heads) and explicit knowledge (in the knowledge bank);
- knowledge communication, capture, storage and retrieval;
- people, process, technology and cultural aspects;
- learning before, during and after;
- project teams and communities of practice.

The rest of this book will look at how this system can be applied to teams and projects.

Cultural issues

We previously discussed how knowledge management requires a profound shift in individual and corporate attitudes to knowledge. In western society, where people are educated through the western system, knowledge is seen as an individual attribute. At school, children are tested on what they know, and any attempt to access the knowledge of others is seen as cheating.[5] In professional life, people often feel a sense of pride in their own skills, knowledge and achievements, and sometimes would rather solve a problem themselves, just for the challenge, than seek for an existing solution. The individual's knowledge and experience can also be felt to be a personal asset, and a hedge against being made redundant, replaced, or outsourced.

When people feel this way, there can be many cultural barriers to knowledge management. These include the following:

- *knowledge is power:* 'if I tell you what I know, I lose some of my personal power';
- *not invented here:* 'your knowledge is not as trustworthy as mine';
- *drive to create:* 'it's more fun finding the answer for myself, than using someone else's answer';
- *fear of exposure:* 'I am not going to share my failures with you, it might make me look bad';
- *fear of exposure (2):* 'I am not going to ask for help and advice, it makes me look as if I don't know what I am doing'.

Any organisation that sees the business value in knowledge management (i.e. reducing the learning curve, bringing everyone up to the best performance standard, as discussed earlier), needs to address these cultural issues. A new culture needs to be developed, as follows:

- *shared knowledge is greater power:* 'if we share what we know, we will meet our individual and strategic targets';
- *invented here is not good enough:* 'we know we don't know everything, and will look around for additional knowledge before every task';
- *drive to perform:* 'it may be more fun to create the solution, but if a better solution exists, we will use it';

- *fear of underperforming:* 'I am going to ask for help and advice, because I want to make my job as easy and safe as possible';
- *fear of underperforming (2):* 'if something went wrong on my project, I am going to make sure it never happens to any future projects'.

The more a team is driven by performance (their own team performance, and also the organisational performance), and empowered to seek solutions, the more readily they will embrace knowledge management, as an aid to performance. Managers can reinforce this, by encouraging and rewarding knowledge-seeking and knowledge-sharing, by setting the expectation that every team will seek to improve on the best of past performance, by empowering teams to seek the best solutions, and by avoiding any internal competition between teams, projects and business units.

Notes

1. 'Heuristics' refers to the rules of thumb, guidelines, working models, and educated guesses which people use to solve problems.
2. One exception is the exchange of knowledge through e-mail dialogue in a shared e-mail forum. Here knowledge can be exchanged between a small number of individuals, but that e-mail exchange can be observed by others, and stored for future reference. More detail of online e-mail forums can be found in Chapter 4.
3. This statement should not be taken as meaning that only people with defined roles should be involved in knowledge management. On the contrary, everyone in the organisation will be involved in knowledge management and learning, but specific assurance roles are needed to make sure the knowledge management systems are applied and followed. The analogy is with safety – everyone in the organisation needs to work in a safe manner, but the accountability for the safety system lies with defined HSSE roles. The absence of these accountabilities is one of the most common reasons for failure of a knowledge management system.
4. There is no point in trying to manage all your knowledge. For much low-value knowledge, the cost of managing it outweighs the value that management will generate. You need to focus on those knowledge areas where the value far outweighs the management cost.
5. There is more of a trend towards course work and group work in western schools today, which may lessen some of the cultural barriers to knowledge sharing in future generations.

Teamwork and project work

In this section we look at the nature of team and project work, in contrast with other ways of working, and how knowledge management can be applied in this specific context.

The team

The most obvious characteristic of teamwork, is that it involves a team. A team is a defined set of individuals, who share collective responsibility for a shared outcome. They bring their skills, knowledge and efforts together in order to deliver a common set of deliverables, through performing a coordinated set of tasks. Through their interactions with the tasks and the project activity, and through their interactions with each other, the individual team members will learn. This individual learning is often unconscious. However, if the team itself is to learn collectively, then learning needs to be discussed and shared between the team members. Team learning cannot be unconscious. Team learning processes are therefore built around dialogue, as discussed in Chapter 3.

When project leaders put a team together, they often look not only at getting the right mix of skills, but also at getting the right mix of personalities. Choosing the right people is crucial if a team is to gel and perform. If the project leader wants to build a learning team, they need to choose team members who are willing to learn. High performing teams will be high-learning teams, and cannot afford to have team members who are not committed to learning. If necessary, people who are resistant to learning may need to leave the team, as described below by the leader of a high-performing team within BP.

> We said that when a person comes on the team they may have to really conform to the team goals and beliefs in order to bed down,

and it happened in three or four occasions where somebody came on board and just did not work out. They could not conform, and we had to ask them to leave.

The initial team-building meeting is the ideal time to start the conversation about knowledge management, for example by inviting the team members to share some of their past experiences, or by combining a peer assist with team building (see Chapter 3).

Some of complexities associated with knowledge management in teams are discussed below.

Multi-company teams

Many projects are joint ventures, or projects involving multiple contractors and sub-contractors. The project teams will therefore be comprised of representatives of many companies, some of which may be competitors in other arenas. Team members may therefore be unwilling to share competitive knowledge with each other, even though knowledge-sharing is critical to the success of the project. There are many issues to be addressed here before the team can start to manage their own knowledge. These include:

- *Issues of misaligned objectives.* The project leader has to work very hard to make sure all parties have goals and objectives which are fully aligned with the success of the project.
- *Issues of terminology.* Exchange of knowledge is hampered when people use different words for the same things. The project leader has to make sure the team develops a common terminology.
- *Issues of technology.* It may be difficult to share documents from one company to another. The project leader has to make sure the team can use a common technology platform, even if this is the lowest common denominator.
- *Issues of secrecy, confidentiality and security.* Sharing knowledge in a multi-company team may feel like an insecure act, unless clear confidentiality guidelines and boundaries are set up.

Virtual teams

Some projects involve a project team which is spread across many countries, and which primarily collaborates virtually rather than face-to-face. The structures and management processes for a project like this are no different from those of a co-located project, but there are additional challenges, as described below by the leader of a global virtual team within BP.

> It's quite a challenge when the core team is a virtual team spread around the world, and it has to be a cohesive and effective team. Communication is a real issue. Time zones are a bit of an issue, also culture and understanding of culture between America and the UK and the different approach these nationalities have.

In knowledge management terms, the project leader will need to make sure that attention is given to communication protocols, and to the development of a common team culture and terminology. Virtual teams tend to highlight the need for certain behaviours, such as openness, clear and frequent communication, and personal commitments to delivery. They also tend to highlight the need to put clear objectives and roles in place, including objectives and roles for knowledge management.

Team culture

Team culture is critical for developing a high-performing, high-learning team with an efficient use of knowledge. Some of the critical cultural elements include:

- *Performance focus*. The team must be driven by performance, and must feel ownership of the performance targets. The drive to perform creates a drive to learn.

- *Empowerment*. The team must feel empowered to do what is necessary (within defined boundaries) to deliver the project, including seeking for knowledge.

- *Openness*. The team members must be fully frank and honest with each other, and they must be willing to learn from other teams and projects, and to re-use existing knowledge.

- *Networking*. The team must be prepared to use knowledge and resources from their personal and company networks in order to deliver the project.

If your team culture is wrong – if the elements mentioned above are absent – then you need to do some cultural work before knowledge management will be effective. Although knowledge management processes such as after action review, peer assist, technical limit, business driven action learning and retrospects (all discussed in detail in Chapter 3) are all themselves culture-change agents, you may also want to invest in some team coaching in order to accelerate the development of the necessary culture.

The defined outcome

The most obvious characteristic of project work, is that it exists to deliver a defined outcome, whether that outcome is an oil well, a completed factory, a new road, a research report, a piece of working software, or a winning bid. Any time there is a defined outcome, knowledge is important. The more you can access the know-how associated with delivering that outcome – knowing how to drill a well, build a factory, construct a road, write a report, develop software or submit a winning bid – the easier and less risky that delivery becomes. 'It's easy when you know how'. Access that know-how, and the outcome becomes easy to deliver.

Some of the characteristics of delivering the project outcome are outlined below.

Defined deliverables

Another characteristic of project work is that it has a beginning and an end. The project ends when the objectives of the project have been delivered to predetermined standards. There must be an outcome, and the outcome must be measurable, so that the project can be defined as complete. Sometimes the deliverables are actual structures, such as pipelines, roads, or factories, while sometimes they are more abstract such as assessments, audits, systems, software or change processes. In every case, however, there will be defined objectives for the projects, and some measure of satisfaction that the project needs to meet. This measure is usually defined by (or together with) the project client. The fact that projects have a defined end with defined deliverables means that there is a natural end-point for collecting knowledge and an outcome to measure performance against, with any deviation from planned performance signifying a learning opportunity.

The project client

Projects are commissioned by someone, or some body such as a board. This person or body is the client. They provide the money, and define the measures of satisfaction. They are involved in discussions or negotiations over the budget, the timescale and the deliverables, and at the end of the day they determine whether or not the project was a success. There may be many stakeholders associated with a project, but there is (or should be) only one client.

The client can be involved in the knowledge management process to an extent, but generally knowledge management should be kept within the team. The best role for the client is to set the expectation that knowledge will be managed in the project.

A defined duration

The fact that projects have a clear duration – a beginning, a middle and an end – is one of the things that sets them apart from other forms of work (discussed later in this chapter). This duration gives a structure to the activity, and knowledge management can be set within that structure. The defined duration of projects allows learning to be divided into 'learning before, during and after' (see Figure 1.6). Projects are often divided into stages (discussed later in this chapter), also of defined duration, and smaller-scale learning cycles can be embedded into these stages. Processes for learning before, during and after are described in Chapter 3.

A work breakdown structure

The project team will deliver the objectives of the project by performing and coordinating a whole series of interrelated tasks. Sometimes the tasks are grouped into subprojects which form components of the main project. The organisation of tasks and subprojects is known as the work breakdown structure. The example in Figure 2.1 is from an oil company. Here the project 'prepare for drilling' consists of four sub-projects, three of which contain more than one distinct task.

The work breakdown structure defines the objectives and assignments for which the members of the project team will be held accountable. In this example, a sub-set of the project team will be assigned the objective of delivering a well plan. They will run this as a sub-project, within which the three main tasks will be coordinated. The geologists will be

Figure 2.1   Example work breakdown structure

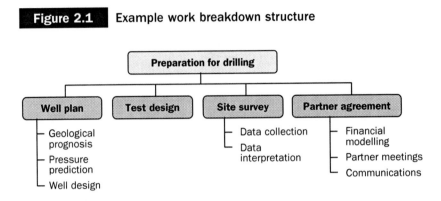

accountable for delivering the geological prognosis, the petroleum engineers for delivering the pressure prediction, and the drilling engineers for delivering the well design.

Knowledge management within the project can also be broken down according to the work breakdown structure. Knowledge management processes can be applied to sub-projects, and the individual tasks within the project are areas of activity where knowledge is created and knowledge is used. Lessons can be accessed and captured at task level (e.g. how to predict pressure) and at subproject level (e.g. how to plan a well). The link between knowledge and performance discussed in the previous chapter must be extended to cover the performance of the subprojects and individual tasks within the work breakdown structure.

Single point accountabilities

The project structure, and the work breakdown structure within the project, are used to set accountabilities. The project leader is accountable for delivering the project. The project team members are jointly responsible for the project, but the single point of accountability lies with the project leader. The project leader can assign accountabilities for subprojects to individual subproject leaders, and accountabilities for individual activities and tasks are assigned to individual members of the project team. This structure of accountability for delivery, and accountability for performance, needs to be matched by a structure of accountabilities for learning (as discussed in Chapter 3).

Project management

Project management is the key management discipline for project work. It involves the coordination of all the resources available for the project, and all of the activities required by the project, in order to best deliver the project objectives. Project management may include the following subsidiary disciplines:

- project scoping and objectives setting;
- people management and contractor management;
- task planning, scheduling and integration;
- cost management and budgeting;
- activity management;
- financial management;
- quality management;
- communications;
- risk management;
- procurement and contracting;
- knowledge management.

Knowledge is one of the key resources within the project, and the management of knowledge has to be included within the project management discipline, just like the management of other project resources such as people or finances. Chapter 5 discusses how this can be done.

A staged approach to projects

A common approach to the management of projects is to divide them into a series of discrete stages, with an explicit high-level decision needed to pass through the stage-gate from one stage to the next. As a project progresses through the stages, the team develops a better understanding of the parameters of the project and of the solution they will develop, and investment decisions can be made progressively. This avoids, for example, commitment to a defined timescale and budget before the problem is sufficiently well defined, or before the project options are fully addressed and reviewed.

A project will generally pass through a number of stages. For example, in a construction project, the following stages are common (other staged schemes are shown in Figure 2.2).

Figure 2.2 **Example stage-gate frameworks**

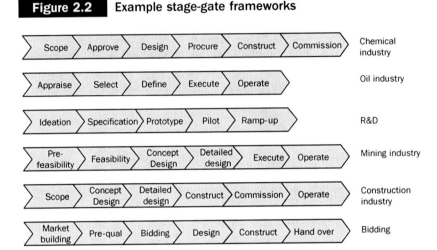

- A stage where the problem, or need, is investigated until it is fully understood. This could be termed the 'scoping', 'pre-feasibility' or 'appraisal' stage. At the end of this stage, the team should have a good idea of the nature of the problem to be solved, whether this is a river to be crossed, or a deepwater oil field to be developed, or user requirements to be fulfilled.

- A stage where the options for the solution are generated and assessed, and a preferred option or concept is selected. This could be called the 'select' or 'approve' or 'specification' or 'concept design' stage. For example, in this stage you might select a suspension bridge option, or a tension-leg platform option, having fully assessed, ranked and rejected the other options.

- A design stage, where the selected option or concept is designed in detail.

- A construction, or execution, stage, where the design is constructed.

- A commissioning or handover phase, when the completed structure or product is handed over.

- An operation phase, usually occurring after the project, when the completed product, structure or system is in use by the customer.

The major advantage of operating a staged approach is that the decision making is also staged. Funds are committed to the project gradually, rather than all at once, and decisions are not made until there is sufficient information and knowledge to make the correct decision. At the end of a stage, the decision is made either to progress, to do more work to complete the stage, or to abort the project.

As the project team goes through the stages, the project will be defined in increasing detail, and increasingly detailed knowledge will be needed. New knowledge will be needed – knowledge of design will be needed in the design stage, knowledge of construction in the construction stage, and knowledge of handover in the handover stage.[1] In fact, the members of the project team may change from one stage to the next, introducing issues of knowledge handover between the stages.

In practice, all projects benefit from a staged approach. Knowledge management within the project must also be staged, with the right knowledge being sought and applied at the right times. The learn before, during and after cycle of Figure 1.6 can be applied at stage level, with a greater degree of focus on immediate needs, rather than attempting to apply it to the entire project. Chapter 3 will address the management of knowledge within a staged project, and Chapter 5 will introduce the concept of a knowledge management plan as a management document.

Construction projects

Construction projects traditionally use a staged approach. Part of the complication of major construction projects is that the different project stages may be handled by different companies. The conceptual design and detailed design stages may be handled by an architect, the construction phase by a civil engineering contractor (or a shipyard, in the case of marine construction), and the operation phase by a different contractor. This adds two extra dimensions to knowledge management, which need to be consciously addressed.

The first is the issue of knowledge sharing between different companies (which may have different terminologies, different cultures, different processes and different technology), and the second is the transfer of knowledge from one project stage to the next. This involves not only transferring knowledge to the subsequent stage (e.g. transferring knowledge from the construction phase to the operation phase), but also the transfer of knowledge to previous stages (e.g. using the knowledge of the operators to construct a better product, and the knowledge of the construction contractor to develop a better design). This is often hampered by the habit of not appointing the contractors until relatively late on in the project, even though their knowledge may have been very useful earlier on.

Research and development projects

Research and development projects are concerned with developing new technology that will (hopefully) have commercial application. The stages of R&D projects typically concern prototyping and piloting, prior to roll-out of the new product. The earliest stages of an R&D project, which look at the development of the potentially marketable product, require the combination of knowledge from a wide number of areas. Technical knowledge is needed, and many new ideas come from a new combination of disparate technical knowledge, such as the combination of biology and mechanics to develop biomechanics. However, the project also needs access to market knowledge, knowledge of customer needs, and knowledge of the development, manufacture and marketing cycle.

Projects which involve bidding

Projects which require competitive bidding will contain additional stages. Before the project can even start, the bid has to be won. However, to construct a winning bid, the bid preparation team needs very good knowledge not only of the customer's requirements and the innovative technologies that can be applied, but also of the practical constraints to project delivery. In addition the team needs sophisticated knowledge about the bidding process itself.

Other types of work

Not every activity in every organisation is delivered by teams, or organised into project frameworks. There are many other types of work, which will have their own particular attributes as far as knowledge management is concerned.

Individual providers and individual contributors

There are very many business activities where people work individually, and not in teams. They may be salesman, customer representatives, internal consultants in an organisation, groundsmen and greenkeepers, teachers, doctors, farmers, and so on. Each of these people is individually accountable for delivering their own performance. They do not share objectives with others. They do not need to collaborate. As far as knowledge management is concerned, they are accountable for seeking, applying, capturing and sharing their own knowledge. However, they may well find it valuable to operate within communities of practice (see Chapter 4), so that they can share knowledge with other individual providers (salesman sharing knowledge with salesman, teachers sharing knowledge with teachers, doctors sharing knowledge with doctors). Even if you are an individual worker, managing your individual knowledge, you can still access and use collective knowledge from the community, and you can still offer your knowledge as a resource that others can use.

Service work

Much of the work of an organisation may involve people who provide a service to the customers (either internal customers, or external customers). For example, a help desk providing a service to dial-in customers, fire crews who respond to emergencies in the community, or health centres and hospitals that provide medical services. This sort of service work is not organised into projects, because to a large extent it is reactive to the needs of the customers. Performance is important, and service providers often agree service levels with the customer, or set themselves performance targets. Some service providers work as individual contributors (see above), while others work in service teams. Many of the principles of knowledge management can be applied to service work, but service work lacks the project framework structure within which knowledge management can be embedded. Service work has no final deliverables, often has no beginning or end (therefore making it difficult to apply learning before, during and after), and requires a different approach to knowledge management.

Knowledge management for service work is concerned with just-in-time provision of knowledge to the service teams, a system of knowledge capture during and after service activity, communities of practice for developing and sharing common approaches, and the development of standards and best practices. There is a very valid and important role to be played by knowledge management for service work, but it won't be covered by this particular book.

Operations work

Operations work – sometimes known as '24/7' – involves working at something that doesn't stop. Working in a factory, a manufacturing operation, operations in a refinery or a pipeline or a pumping station, are all ongoing activities. They have no start, no middle and no end (except on the scale of the lifetime of the factory or refinery itself). Operators may work as individual contributors (see above), or they may work in operations teams. However, they do not work in a project framework. They have no project end to work towards, and no discrete deliverables other than ongoing performance targets. Their approach to knowledge management is therefore different from that of the project worker, because there is no project framework within which to embed the knowledge management activities.

There is usually a very strong focus on performance in operational activity. Operational teams have targets, which usually concern quality, throughput, reliability and uptime. Performance is measured on a regular basis, whether this is daily, weekly or monthly. Production targets, or quality targets, are also set on a regular basis. It is this performance management cyclicity that can provide the framework for embedding knowledge management. Operational teams can learn before, during and after each performance management cycle, and this is the equivalent to a project team learning before, during and after each project stage.

Operational knowledge management can also benefit from benchmarking across the operations. For a company with more than one factory, for example, it should be possible to benchmark key performance indicators such as quality, performance and reliability. The good performers can be identified and encouraged to analyse their performance, draw out the good practices, and share their knowledge. The poor performers can be encouraged to seek and apply these good practices. The factories can be given the collective target of improving their collective performance, and collectively rewarded for any improvement. Benchmarking can drive performance, which can drive learning and knowledge management.

However, to be able to benchmark effectively across operations, the organisation will need standard metrics and standard key performance indicators, which can be objectively applied across all the operations. There may also need to be some sort of audit, to make sure that performance is being measured in a consistent way. They will also need a culture that sees benchmarking as a means to drive improvement, rather than an excuse for punishing failure.

Operational knowledge management also strongly benefits from the establishment of communities of practice (Chapter 4) for the peer exchange of knowledge across the operations. Operators across the organisation can use each other as a resource for solving problems and identifying good practices.

There is a very valid and important role to be played by knowledge management for operational and service work, but it will need to be described in the next book.

Note

1. This is, of course, simplistic. Consideration needs to be give to, for example, commissioning and hand-over as early as the design stage, or even earlier. However more, and more detailed, knowledge will be needed for each stage as each stage is approached.

The flow of knowledge within projects

In Chapter 1, and in Figure 1.6, we introduced the model of learning before, during and after project activity. This concept is at the heart of understanding the flow of knowledge within projects.

Each project, and each stage of each project, will need to import knowledge. Knowledge will be needed to deliver the project stage, and the tasks and activities within that stage. The project team will need to learn before they start, in order to access the knowledge they need.

As the project stages continue, the project team will learn as they go. Some processes are needed for capturing that knowledge, and taking action to improve team performance based on the new knowledge.

At the end of each project stage, the new knowledge that has been gained needs to be identified and captured, for passing on to the next stage, or for passing on to other projects.

At each stage therefore, the knowledge needs to be imported, gathered, applied, captured, documented and exported. This section looks at learning before, during and after, and how these principles may be applied during the various project stages.

Learning before

Learning before a piece of activity involves:

- identifying the knowledge which will be useful to the project team in helping them deliver the project objectives;
- identifying the sources of that knowledge (both explicit and tacit), and
- doing something to bring the knowledge into the team.

The team will probably have some of this knowledge already – they would not have been picked for the team without some previous

Figure 3.1 Potential learning before activities in the project stages

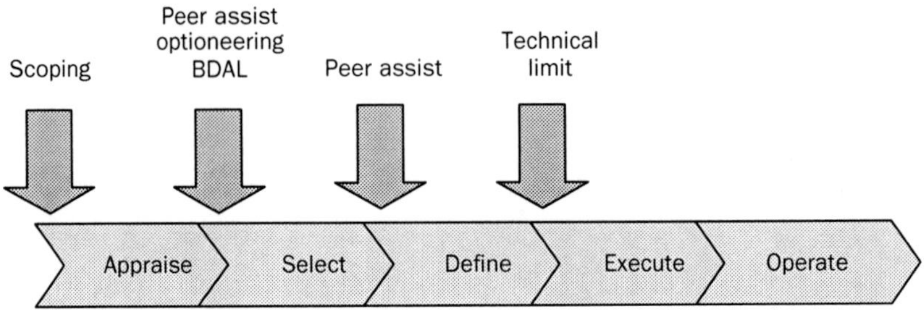

experience and skills. However, even the best team does not have access to all the knowledge and experience. One of the early steps in each project stage must be to maximise the team's access to useful knowledge, so they can start work further down the learning curve[1] (see Chapter 1).

One of the tasks of the project manager will be to develop a culture within the team where learning before doing is seen as a positive activity, rather than a sign of weakness. Sometimes teams are reluctant to seek for help and advice, in case it seems as if they don't know what they are doing. However, the chances are that there are some very useful lessons and solutions available to the team, if they took the time to look for them. Why reinvent the wheel, if a perfectly good wheel exists already? Why repeat mistakes, or re-tackle issues, if perfectly good solutions exist?

The following sections look at 'learning before' activities in the different project stages, some of which are shown in Figure 3.1.

Learning before in the scope/appraise stage

The first stage of a project is all about understanding the problem that needs to be solved. The team needs to understand the customer's (or client's) needs and aspirations, the customer needs to understand the range of what is possible, and all parties need to understand the constraints (environmental, legal, technological) under which the project will operate.

Outputs from this stage will be the strategic objectives of the project, a first-pass risk analysis, and potentially a first-pass cost and time estimate.

The knowledge at this stage will be 'knowledge about' the project and the issues, rather than 'know-how' of how to execute the project. This knowledge will reside mostly at a high organisational level, in the client, the customer, the project manager, the managers of any major contractors, senior advisors, and so on. Much of this knowledge transfer will be face-to-face, as the knowledge will largely be tacit.

Figure 3.2 suggests that two areas of knowledge are needed: knowledge of what needs to be done in the project, and knowledge of how to do it. In the scope/appraise stages of the project, the team will be seeking to maximise their knowledge of what needs to be done. Knowledge of 'how to do it' comes later. The enemy of project clarity, in the early stages, tends to be assumptions – assumptions by the client that they know what they need, and assumptions within the project team that they know what the client needs. A project team who really knows what the really needs, is in a better position to deliver a successful project than a team who thinks they know what the client thinks they want.

Scoping meetings

A technique for surfacing and applying knowledge in the early stages of a project, is the *scoping* meeting (also known as *right-scoping, alignment* or *objective-setting* meetings). Whatever it is called, this meeting is intended to make sure that both the customer and project team clearly know what the project needs to deliver. At this meeting, the customer and the project team come together, to clearly identify and document the purpose of the project, and the strategic value to the organisation. The

Figure 3.2   The two axes of knowledge

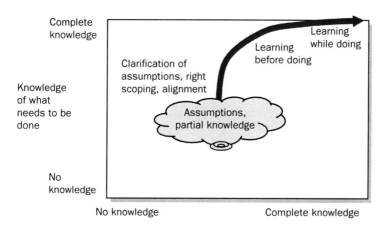

Knowledge of how to do it

question being answered is 'what is this project really for? What will it do for us?'. Failure to clarify the answer to this question is a common reason for projects going off the rail, and lessons about lack of clarity are commonly heard at project retrospects.

Once you have a clear idea of the purpose, the value drivers and the performance indicators, then you can start to set clear objectives which will deliver the value. These objectives ideally should be expressed in functional terms rather than technical terms. For example, taking a core sample is a technical objective, whereas the functional objectives might be to understand the mineralogy and metal content of the ore body. If you express the objectives in a functional way, then it does not presuppose the methodology by which you will deliver the objectives. Decide what you want, before deciding how to achieve it.

The objective-setting process should be by consensus and not by conflict, and you want all the core project team to buy into the objectives fully. This means that the objectives should be as clear as possible, with no ambiguity. The customer and the team need to be clear which objectives are set in stone, and which are (if push comes to shove) negotiable.

Example purpose and strategic objectives for an oilfield development project might be as follows:

Purpose

- To fill the gap in oil production forecast for 2008.

Strategic objectives

- To deliver first oil by 12/12/2007
- To meet regulatory targets
- Zero environmental or safety incidents;
- Zero gas flaring
- 80 per cent local involvement in construction (negotiable)
- Zero CO_2 discharges (aspiration).

These objectives do not, at this stage, presuppose how the project will be designed or constructed. An excellent method for surfacing the knowledge of what is needed, is *customer interview*.

Customer interview

Never assume you or the customers know precisely what is needed or wanted. Talk about it and seek absolute clarity before proceeding. In a clearly defined project, the customer (or client) is often very clear about what needs to be done, and why. In less well-defined projects, or in subprojects within a larger project, that clarity may sometimes be lacking. Also, that clarity is not always communicated to the project team. The client may tacitly know what they need, but not have expressed this explicitly, either to themselves or to the project team. Customer interview is a dialogue technique for making this knowledge explicit.

The following questions are very useful during customer interview:

- What's missing now, that means we have to do this work?
- What do we want to be able to do afterwards, that we can't do now?
- Why do we consider this to be an opportunity?
- What are the customer's conditions of satisfaction?
- How will the customer (and the project team) know if the project has been a success?
- What will the results of this project be used for, and by whom?
- What business environmental factors do we need to be aware of?

An alternative technique of customer interview consists of asking the 'five whys'. This involves asking 'why' as often as necessary (five times is generally sufficient) and is best explained by an example, taken from a customer interview at the start of a project to update a database of risks and volumes.

Q: *Why* do we need to update the database?

A: Because the information is no longer up to date.

Q: But *why* do we need the information to be up-to-date?

A: In order to understand the size of our inventory.

Q: *Why* do we need to know the size of the inventory?

A: Because we report it; at the quarterly performance reviews.

Q: *Why* do we need to report it?

A: Because the business unit leader's performance contract contains items specific to the size of the prospect inventory, and he needs to be able to report against this.

By this process it became clear that the project was supporting assurance of the business unit leader's performance contract, rather than just keeping a database up-to-date. Maybe the database was not the best way to do this. Similar clarification can generally be reached on any project through customer interview.

Ideation and innovation

The early stages of R&D projects are also about defining the problem, but the problem may be rather wider than the known needs of an identified customer. Sometimes R&D will be focused on innovative solutions to a known problem, but at other times it may be looking for innovate products to create a new market. The project therefore may seek to deliver an opportunity rather than solve a problem.

The knowledge which is needed at the ideation stage includes knowledge of possible technologies, and knowledge of the users of the technology (or of the customer market for the new technology). The team may also need knowledge of the regulatory framework, and (in the case of development of new products) they may need knowledge of the manufacturing and distribution process. There is no point in developing new technology if you don't also consider how it will be marketed and sold.

A customer interview will not be sufficient to define the scope of the project, and the team may need to consider options such as scenario planning, where they get together and discuss:

- If we developed this form of technology, who would use it?
- How would they use it?
- What value would it add to them?
- Could we market it?
- Would we need to change the way we operated?
- What risks would it bring?
- What other opportunities would it bring?
- What would happen if we didn't develop it?

Bidding

When the project needs to be acquired through competitive bidding, then it is difficult to conduct any form of customer interview, although in some instances you are allowed dialogue before or after the invitation to tender (ITT) is issued. The project may have to acquire knowledge of the customer's needs through careful analysis of the supplied documentation (such as the request for proposal), through any access they may have to the customer (e.g. question and answer sessions), and through any background knowledge they can gain on the customer and his business. Additional knowledge they need includes:

- knowledge of the bidding process (how best to construct a winning bid);
- knowledge of how best to construct a bid for that customer;
- knowledge of competitors and what they may bid;
- knowledge about the customer and the service they need/want;
- detailed knowledge of what it might be possible to deliver.

Involvement of contractors

Knowledge is also brought into the project in their heads of the project team members. Each member of the team will have their own knowledge and experience which can be brought to bear on the project. Often these project team members come from different companies (such as the major contractors), and each can bring their own company insight. On larger projects, a common historical practice is not to appoint some of the major contractors until later in project life. For example, the construction contractor may not be identified until after the scoping phase or even the concept selection phase, and may only join the team during the construction phase. This approach has one advantage, and one major disadvantage. The advantage is that the project can go out to competitive tender after the project has been relatively well-defined, and so can usually secure very competitive rates. The major disadvantage is that the construction contractor probably has more experience than anybody about how best to design and construct the project, and this experience is most valuable in the early stages. If the major contractors are brought together early in the project, they can very often suggest alternative solutions which can significantly improve the project.

A major company recently commissioned a project for a radical redesign and conversion of an old ship, in order to use it for a new purpose. By involving the architects and the shipyard at the early stages of concept selection and design, they were able to identify many shortcuts to the process, and to use the collective knowledge and experience of all three parties to deliver a far better project plan. At the end of the project, the conversion was complete and the ship set sail five months ahead of deadline, and entirely to specification. The quotes below show how useful it was to bring in the contractors' knowledge early in the process, and how it might have been even better to involve them even earlier.

> The fact that we (the architects) were in with the project from the beginning allowed us to get to know the ship long before the drawings were needed. In a job like this we should be involved at the concept stage. (Naval Architect Representative)

> We should have made the decision and got people on board even earlier, in the pre-feasibility stage. The benefits of getting people together early are immeasurable. (Project Manager)

> We sat for the first time in August, and just in that week we saved a month on the programme. We should have established a team earlier than August; we should have got the shipyard involved in the feasibility or class two study. (Project team member)

The money you might save by going through competitive tendering could easily be offset by the value of the knowledge that the contractors could bring into the project in the early stages. This trade-off needs to be discussed by the project team right from the outset.

Before the concept select/concept design stage

If we can assume that the team has gained sufficient knowledge of the problem which needs to be addressed, and of the needs and strategic objectives of the customer, then the next project stage is concerned with selecting the right option for project delivery. At a high level, the team are starting to require knowledge on how to best tackle this sort of project. They will want to know:

- Who has done this sort of thing before, and how successful were they?
- What options have been tried in the past?
- What are the advantages and disadvantages of those options?
- What are the issues we need to consider in selecting an option?
- What is the best option for us going forward?
- What risks and opportunities will this option bring?

The knowledge that the team needs will be held by a variety of people, including:

- project leaders and project teams from previous projects;
- the current project team;
- people or companies who will join the team during the detailed design and construction stages.

This knowledge can be brought into the project in a number of ways, some of which are described below.

Peer assist

A peer assist is a meeting where the project team invites people with relevant knowledge and experience, to come and share it with the project team. Peer assists are one of the simplest and most effective ways of bringing tacit knowledge into the team, they are so effective that many organisations, such as BP and De Beers, are making them mandatory for major projects. The success of peer assists depends on the following factors.

- The peer assist needs clear objectives. The peers are bringing their knowledge to the team, for a purpose. The clearer you can be about that purpose, the more likely it is that the peer assist will deliver value. Sample objectives might be 'Develop a list of risks and issues', or 'Provide a list of options for cutting 50 per cent off the project budget'.
- The peer assist should be focused on assisting. In other words, it is a meeting where the project team asks for help and assistance, which is provided by the visiting peers. The project team therefore needs to be willing to learn, and their peers need to be willing to share their knowledge and experience. If the meeting falls into 'attack and defend' behaviours, then it has failed its purpose. This willingness will be most easily achieved if 1) the peer assist is held early in the stage,

before the team have selected their preferred option, and 2) the peer assist is facilitated by someone external to the project.

- The peer assist should truly involve peers; i.e. the peers of the project team. These are not meetings where you bring in experts or senior managers. Bring in project managers and team members from previous projects, who have experience to share. People are far more open to learning from, and sharing with, their peers, and this removes all the politics associated with management hierarchies.

The ideal structure for a peer assist is a four-part structure.

- In the first part of the meeting, after the introductions and welcome, the project team explains what they know about the project context, the needs of the customer, the strategic objectives, and any local constraints under which they may be working.
- In the second part of the meeting, the peers discuss their knowledge and experience from previous projects.
- In the third part of the meeting, the project team and the visiting peers go though a process of dialogue, often in small groups, as they attempt to use past experience to address the project team's issues.
- In the final part of the meeting, the visiting peers confer, then feed back their recommendations to the project team.

A typical example of an early-stage peer assist comes from an oil company who were looking for ways to cut the cost of constructing petrol stations in Europe. They held a peer assist in the scoping stage of the project, and invited a wide range of people from within the organisation, and from partner organisations, to come and present options for new ways of working. One of the people they invited was from an alliance contractor in a different part in the business, who suggested that one option might be to form an alliance with a building company. The builder could take care of permitting and construction of each petrol station, and then pass on ownership to the oil company once the petrol station was built. When all the options have been investigated and ranked, this one turned out to be the preferred option, the alliance was formed, and has been operating highly successfully ever since.

Optioneering

Optioneering is one form of peer assist, designed to develop and rank a list of options, or conceptual designs, for the project. It involves a session of facilitated brainstorming, and then checking the options against the values and objectives of the project. The project team and a range of selected visitors will go ahead and investigate the options further, in order to select the preferred approach or preferred concept design.

Optioneering needs to start with a restatement of the purpose and values of the project, and of the functional objectives. This is particularly important for the people external to the project who have been invited. The brainstorming part of the optioneering session needs to be open and creative, and it is important that it is facilitated. The idea is to come out with a number of creative and innovative options, rather than to discuss these or make judgments. The outcome of the brainstorming will be a list of possibilities.

These options now need a preliminary ranking, to decide which ones to work further. This is done in two stages.

- First the *selection criteria* are decided. What are the criteria that the options will be selected against? Does the option need to be low risk? Low cost? Quick to deploy? Fit with existing solutions?

- The criteria are listed, and given a *numerical weighting* depending on importance. The numerical weighting is achieved by dividing 100 points between the criteria.

- The options are *compared with the criteria*, and given a score of between 1 and 5 depending on how well they meet the criteria. A score of 5, for example, means that that option fits that criterion very well.

- The *votes are multiplied by the weightings* in order to rank the options. The team sense-checks this ranking to make sure that promising ideas have not been downgraded by conservatism.

- Those options which are considered for taking further are assigned to individuals who will go away, and *analyse them further*.

The outcome of this stage is a list of screened ideas and options, which will be carried forward into analysis by the project team.

Generating and ranking options needs to be done with a full knowledge base, if it is to be done at all. If you don't fully understand the range of options, or if your knowledge of those options is insufficient, then you may not end up with the best option for the project. The optioneering process needs an input of knowledge from the following people:

- the project team, who have a good idea of the issues and the measures of success of the project;
- people with experience and knowledge from elsewhere, who have a good idea of how the options have performed in the past.

Business-driven action learning

If there is sufficient time, or if the project is sufficiently innovative, then a business-driven action learning stage may be needed to bring knowledge into the project. Here the team engage on a programme of collective knowledge gathering, in order to address some of the issues of the project. The team can glean learning from other parts of the business, but more usually they are seeking knowledge from external sources. They can even learn from what their competitors are doing. For example, when BP were opening their first Western-style petrol station in Japan, the team spent some time going round competitors' sites to see what issues they were facing, and how their competitors dealt with them.

Business-driven action learning is often used to bring new knowledge and innovation into a project. For example, when De Beers embarked on a project to develop a new autonomous underwater vehicle for sea-bed imaging, the first stage was to set up a business-driven action learning programme. Here a small team of four spent several months working with universities and suppliers to develop a breakthrough solution.

The keys to success in an action learning programme are as follows.

- The team needs clarity about the topics they need to research. This can be broken down into sub-topics, and individual team members can be given accountability for researching individual sub-topics, but ultimately the emphasis has to be on collective learning.
- The team needs to seek knowledge from six areas:
  - Knowledge creators such as research centres, consultants and academic. Work with the best knowledge source. Be patient and ensure you have identified the right people to work with.
  - Suppliers of technology and services. You need to build highly collaborative partnerships with suppliers and contractors, to fully exploit each other's experience, knowledge and competencies.
  - Regulators, both internal and external.
  - Customers, to understand their needs, using the best user-group you can get to represent the internal and/or external customer population.

- The wider social environment, to learn what will be acceptable as a solution.
- Competitors, to gain as much knowledge as possible of the competitive environment.

■ The team needs to consist of top-quality users who can interface with all the above groups.

■ The team needs to come together on a regular basis for team reflection and team learning. They will use peer assists to capture knowledge, will apply after action reviews (see below) on a daily basis to keep their learning current, and will hold a retrospect (see below) at the end of the business-driven action learning programme. They will package what they have learned into a knowledge asset (Chapter 4).

■ The team needs be trained in the principles of gathering knowledge. They need to be able to interview, to facilitate retrospects and after action reviews, and to express learning in terms of actionable advice for the future. Although the team undoubtedly has the right skills to deliver the project itself, they might not have the right skills for action learning, and they will need some training and coordination.

■ The sources of knowledge, both internal and external, need to be briefed about the purpose of the action learning, and to help the learning team as much as they can. Obviously this won't happen if the team is trying to learn from competitors!

An example of this form of business-driven action learning comes from a team of hospital administrators. They were putting together a bid to construct and operate a hospital, and spent some time going round existing hospitals operated by the same company, to learn as much as they could about the issues of hospital management. They were able to gather lessons about hospital operation which would help them significantly when it came to putting the bid together, and developing the hospital design.

Peer review

Peer review is a process often used in a staged project approach, as a way of reviewing whether a project is ready to go through the stage gate. For example, the project team might call a peer review at the end of the scoping/appraisal stage, as a way of checking that they have fully understood the problem, looked at all the risks, created the necessary project management frameworks (including a knowledge management plan, see Chapter 5), and defined the correct strategic objectives. A group of technical and functional experts are brought in to review progress, and highlight any gaps that need to be filled before going to the stage gate.

Peer review is not really a knowledge management process. Although the peer review panel of experts bring their knowledge and experience to bear when analysing the project, they are not particularly concerned with transferring this knowledge to the project team. Peer review is more of an assurance process than a knowledge process, and is concerned more with independent technical assessment than with the transfer of knowledge to the project team (which is better served by holding the peer assist earlier in the project stage).

Before the define/design stage

In the previous project stage, the team should have looked at all conceptual options for the project, and chosen the best option to take forward. This next project stage is concerned with detailed design. The team are now starting to need quite detailed knowledge about how to design and implement the project. They need to know:

- What precisely is the end product going to look like?
- What are the operational issues that need to be designed in at this stage (e.g. maintenance issues)
- What is the precise series of steps that we will take during construction?
- What are details of the construction/implementation plan?
- What is the benchmark performance in terms of cost, time, quality and safety, and what sort of performance should we aim for?
- What are the main risks and constraints that will face us? How do we address these?

The knowledge that the team needs will be held by a variety of people, including:

- project teams from previous projects;
- the current project team;
- the people (often contractors) who will be involved in construction/implementation;
- the people (often contractors, or customer staff) who will be involved in operating the project after it has been constructed.

This knowledge can be brought into the project in a number of ways, some of which are described below.

Peer assist

A peer assist is often very valuable at the start at the design/define stage, to bring in knowledge from other teams about how to design the project. Details of the peer assist process are described above.

A typical case history for a design-stage peer assist comes from a retail organisation starting up in a new country. The country was Venezuela, and the organisation had taken over a chain of local dealerships. They wanted a business information system in place within six months, but the vendors thought it would take ten months to deliver.

Several other parts of the same organisation had recently installed similar systems, so Venezuela called a two-day peer assist with the objectives of designing a business information system which could be delivered in less than six months. They did some pre-work by video conference, and carefully constructed an agenda to focus on knowledge sharing.

By re-using approaches applied in Poland and Russia, Venezuela were able to build a plan to deliver the system within four months. Not only were able to accelerate their delivery, they also believe costs would have been half a million dollars higher without the peer assist.

Business driven action learning

The business-driven action learning programme described previously can be extended into this project stage.

Technical limit

The technical limit process is a process used within the oil industry, which accesses the detailed practical knowledge of the drilling contractors in order to develop the best possible drilling plan. This process leads up to the technical limit meeting, which is held late in the design stage, immediately before operations, when an outline plan already exists. At the meeting, the knowledge from the drilling contractors is used to refine and optimises plan before starting to drill the well. Technical limit is described below, as it is more about learning before the execution stage, than it is about learning before the design stage, but the ground work for technical limit must be laid earlier in the project.

Involvement of contractors

As discussed above, the contractors should ideally be part of the team at this stage. The construction contractors will be able to add a huge amount of knowledge through the technical limit process (see below), and the contractor or the teams who will take over at the end of the project (the operations and maintenance people for a construction project, the sales and marketing people for an innovation or product creation project) should also be involved as early as possible. Optimising the total lifecycle costs of a project involves taking maintenance issues into account during design.

This early involvement has implications for the contracting strategy.

Learning before the execute/construct phase

The knowledge needed before the execution/construction stage is very practical know-how about the tasks, activities and sub-projects identified on the work breakdown structure of the implementation plan. This knowledge will come from the construction team themselves, and the construction contractor, and also from previous teams and other projects. This is a time of considerable activity, and much of the knowledge will be needed urgently, during the activity, and is discussed below.

A very powerful method of learning before construction phase is the technical limit process, described below.

Technical limit

The process known at BP as 'technical limit', and at Shell as 'drilling the limit', has delivered tremendous value in the oil industry, commonly resulting in a massive leap in performance (Dolan et al., 2003). The concept is relatively simple. It involves using the knowledge and experience of the drilling crews in perfecting the drilling execution plan. Traditionally, the oil company would prepare the drilling plan in the design/define stage of the project, and this would be passed to the drilling contractor who would drill the well during the execute stage. The drilling crews (staff from the drilling contractor who will actually do the work) are usually the people who know best how the work can be done, and by involving them before the execution starts, the oil companies can not only access the knowledge and build a better plan, they can also involve the drilling crews in setting and adopting aggressive performance targets.

The technical limit process consists of the following stages:

- An engagement exercise is needed, so that the project team, project manager, customer and contractors all buy into the use of the process. Because the process involves the contractor in detailed design and in target setting, it requires a different relationship between the contractor and the project team. The contractor needs to feel an equal partner in the project and this has to be thought through carefully when putting the contract together. There is no point in putting in place an adversarial contract with heavy penalty clauses, and then expecting the contractor to freely share their knowledge. Technical limit works best in a partnership or alliance framework, where all parties will benefit if the project is delivered ahead of time or under cost, and all parties suffer equally if deadlines or budgets are not met.

- The project team, project manager and customer need to agree the primary performance indicator for the project. Technical limit will seek to maximise this performance indicator. In the case of drilling projects, the primary performance indicator is time. If a well is drilled faster, the oil will be produced sooner, and also the drilling costs will be lower (as drilling rigs are hired by the day, and are very expensive). In other projects, the primary driver might be cost rather than time.

- During the design stage of the project, the project team divide the project plan into the smallest possible component activities and tasks. For example, the drilling plan may be divided into several hundred steps, each of which will take between half an hour and a day to complete.

- The project team collects performance data on all of these steps. This is relatively easy in the drilling industry, where detailed performance records are kept. The team is looking to find the best performance for each of these steps, as well as the average performance.

- Just before operations start, the project team calls a technical limit meeting, and invites the drilling crews, and all the other contractors who will be involved in the execution (drilling) stage of the project. They present this detailed breakdown of activity and performance.

- The meeting breaks into small break-out groups who go through the plan step by step. For each step they ask three questions.
  - 'Do we need to do this step?'
  - 'If we do need to do it, can we take it off the critical path?'
  - 'If this step is on the critical path, how can we do it as quickly as possible? What needs to be in place to deliver best performance?'

- They also look at the risks involved with any changes to the programme, and they also set a target time for each step. This target time should be at least as quick as the best historical performance. For example, if a previous team on a similar project could run the anchors in eight hours, then there is no reason why this team should not run the anchors just as quickly.
- This revised plan, and revised performance targets, are then taken forward into the execution stage, and reviewed on a daily basis (as described under 'learning during').

Typically a drilling team may find they can save 10–20 per cent of operational time by taking tasks off the critical path or by eliminating them altogether, and an additional 10–20 per cent operational time by optimising the tasks that remain.

The technical limit process has been used in other industries, not just the oil industry. For example, it was applied very successfully recently to a mine delineation project – a project involving sinking a number of boreholes into an underground ore body to delineate the size and shape of the resource. A technical limit meeting was held, and the team started working through the detailed plan with the contractor staff, looking at each step, and looking for ways to eliminate them or do them faster.

One of the early steps for each borehole was to cement in a pipe, and wait six hours for the cement to set. When they worked through the process, the contractor said that this step wasn't necessary, as the pipe would be so jammed in with mud and gravel that it would not need cementing. They only cemented in the pipes because the customer specified this in the contract. When the customer was asked why this was in the contract, they said they had put it in because they assumed the step was necessary. So both parties were happy to leave out the cementing step, thus saving six hours per borehole on a programme of nearly 50 boreholes (a total time saving of two weeks on the entire programme). And this was only one step out of several dozen.

Learning before the operate stage

The transfer of knowledge from the construction stage to the operate stage, involves knowledge about whatever it is the project produced; the new factory, the new hospital, the new oil well, the new product, the new software. As there is now a major change in activity – from constructing to operating – there will be little transfer of know-how. The operators don't need to know how to construct; they need to know how to operate and maintain. However, there will be a lot of transfer of other forms of knowledge and information, such as operating procedures, plans, designs, layouts etc.

One of the best ways of transferring knowledge of a factory or plant to the operations and maintenance team is to involve them in the commissioning and handover stages (in fact, even before commissioning starts), so that they transfer learning about the plant 'on the job'.

Learning during

Learning during the project involves making sure that new knowledge is captured on a routine basis, that new lessons are discussed with the project team, and that new learnings are sought and applied in the project to overcome issues and obstacles. Learning during processes are applied consciously and regularly in order to bring the team up to full speed as fast as possible. The knowledge can come from within the project team, as they 'learn while doing', or it can come from outside the project team, to help the team solve problems and reduce risks.

Learning during the different project stages

The size of the team, and the intensity of activity, will determine how much attention needs to be paid to learning during. A big and busy team, working on new activity and learning rapidly during the execution/ construction stage of the project, needs to capture knowledge on a daily basis. A smaller design team, or project definition team, in the early stages of a project may not need to share knowledge so often.

Some learning during processes are listed below.

After action reviews

After action reviews (AARs) are applied in many industries as a mechanism for learning during project activity. They are focused review meetings, relatively short in duration, designed to help the team become conscious of their own knowledge, so they can act on that knowledge as work progresses. It is like 'learning on Tuesday to perform better on Wednesday'. In addition, the learning can be transferred to other teams, but this is generally a secondary role.

This process was developed by the US Army, who use it as their main knowledge-gathering process. It does not go into very great analytical depth, and so is useful for reviewing short-turnaround activity, or single actions. It is short and focused enough to do on a daily basis, perhaps at the end of a meeting or at the end of a shift. For example, a refining company might use AARs after each shift during maintenance activity.

More detailed, longer-duration knowledge capture exercises will be needed at the end of project stages. Some companies use the term *after action review* for both the short focused, and the long detailed, processes, but this can be confusing, so in this book we use the term *retrospects* for the longer, detailed exercise (see below).

The structure of an AAR is very simple. It consists of asking the four questions listed below. The questions are answered through dialogue within the team.

1. *What was supposed to happen?* The first question is asked about the objective of the activity, and the target performance. We have often found that the first few times you ask this question, people may turn out to have been confused about the objective or the target, or else no clear objective was set. One of the by-products of AARs is that they promote clear objective-setting.

2. *What actually happened?* The second question looks at actual performance. If you are conducting an AAR, you need to establish 'ground truth' with this question. You are looking to determine reality, rather than opinion.

3. *Why was there a difference?* The third question seeks to understand why a particular result was achieved. Perhaps you did better than expected; perhaps you did worse than expected; perhaps you met your target. What were the factors that determined the result? What were the root causes? Another way to ask this question, if the first way doesn't work, is '*What went well, and what did not go so well?*' The US Army AARs sometimes ask for '*three up, three down*' – i.e. three items that worked better than expected, and three items that worked worse than expected.

4. *What have we learned?* The final question asks about the learning, and should be expressed in terms of what will be done differently the next day (or, in cases of over-performance, what should be repeated the next day). Here you move from analysis of the activity, to 'what are we going to do about it'.

The answers to these questions can usefully be recorded on a one-page pro forma (or a marked up flip chart – Figure 3.3), which can be collected for future reference.

An example AAR from a refinery maintenance exercise follows, and shows the level of task detail to which AARs may be applied. This example comes from a shift team in Singapore, who were installing trays within a refinery unit (a tray is a particular piece of equipment inside a refinery column, and needs to be fitted by someone working at height).

- *What was supposed to happen?* (1) To install trays, with weir heights and downcomers within tolerance. (2) To hold tray assembly in place with appropriate hardware, e.g. bolts and nuts, clamps, washers, slide fasteners, etc.

- *What actually happened?* (1) Tray clearances were not within tolerance. (2) There was a shortage of hardware.

- *Why was there a difference?* (1) Workers were using measuring tapes to adjust the clearances resulting in a need for repeated re-working. (2) Workers were transporting the hardware up the column in bulk,

Figure 3.3   Flip chart marked up for an AAR

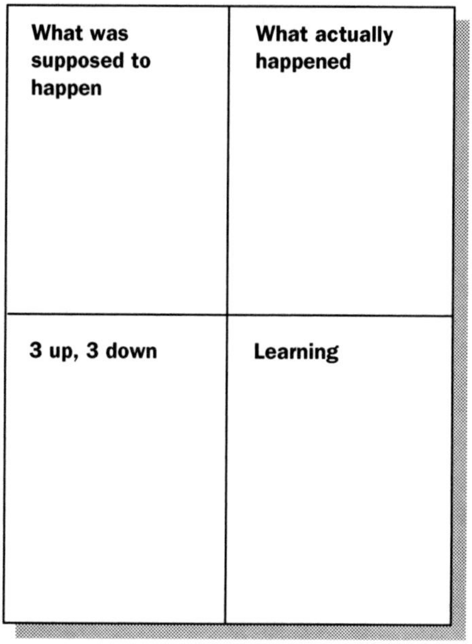

What was supposed to happen	What actually happened
3 up, 3 down	Learning

resulting in hardware being misplaced, dropped, or not following vendor's instruction on the appropriate type of hardware to be used.

- *What have we learned?* (1) Use standard blocks prepared to the required dimensions for adjusting weir height and downcomer clearance. (2) Put all the appropriate hardware in place on the tray sections at ground level before transporting up the column.

Although the learning here is only about small things – tray tolerances, clamps and washers – an increased ability to avoid small mistakes, based on day-by-day routine learning, can give a massive performance improvement at the end of the project.

The AAR process works well in an open, blame-free, inclusive environment. You need to set the ground rules for AARs, and some of the rules are as follows:

- aim for openness, not hiding any mistakes;
- there should be no hierarchy – everyone's input is equally valid;
- the focus of the exercise is learning, not blame or evaluation;
- everyone who was involved in the activity should take part in the AAR;
- no outsiders should be present, nobody should be there to audit performance;
- deal with the significant issues and the significant objectives, not trivia.

After action reviews fit very well with target setting, and form a natural continuation to the technical limit process (see below).

After action reviews and technical limit

During the technical limit process, the project will have been divided into many small steps, and the operational team (the drilling crew, in the oil industry examples) will have set themselves performance targets for each step. This divides the project into a level of granularity which is appropriate for learning during using AARs (see comments in Chapter 1).

During operations, the technical limit process needs to be continued, with continued emphasis on meeting targets, and continued capture of lessons to help improvement. Targets will have been set, through the technical limit process, for each piece of activity. At the end of the day, or the end of the activity, the teams use an AAR to compare performance with the target. So on an oil rig, the driller might call the crew together and say 'we set ourselves a target of doing this task in nine hours. It actually took twelve. Why was there a difference, and what have we learned?' The team themselves act on any learnings they can, and keep an action log to record changes to the drilling plan. Any lessons that need to be escalated are collected and reported back to the onshore office every morning during the morning telephone report, then entered into the project lessons database.

Communities of practice

During project activity, teams may face unexpected problems and challenges, and may need rapid access to knowledge from their peers elsewhere in the organisation. This is best achieved by linking the team members with their respective communities of practice.

Communities of practice are peer networks of practitioners within an organisation, who help each other perform better by sharing their knowledge. For example, a community of practice might be set up for electrical engineers, so that engineers can raise issues and problems, and ask if anyone in the community can provide insights and suggest solutions. Many of the larger companies have set up dozens of communities of practice, some of which may have over a thousand members. Communities generally have a facilitator or moderator, and may sometimes have a more sophisticated governance system. Community members exchange knowledge in two ways. They can capture and share good practice documents, or they can use a 'questions and answers' forum to ask one another for help and advice.

Communities can be a tremendous resource for project teams, especially during the construction/execution stage. If the team hits unexpected problems, they can request help from the community, and hope that someone in the community can provide a solution, or useful advice. Communities can be a resource to the team for 'learning before', but come into their own while 'learning during'. They provide 'just-in-time' access to the tacit knowledge within the community. For example, one project-based organisation maintains an active 'cost and schedule network', which acts as a community of practice for the project services professionals. Any project services manager with an issue relating cost estimating or scheduling can contact the network for help, support, advice, benchmark statistics, and good practice.

Communities of practice are usually set up for specific practice areas or disciplines, so in different organisations you might find communities of marine engineers, software designers or drillers. In a multidisciplinary project team, the individual discipline practitioners should each be an active member of their respective communities of practice, in order to access knowledge on behalf of the project. So the team delivering the task shown in Figure 2.1 needs to be linked into a community of drillers, a community of geologists, a community of surveyors, a community of financial planners etc. The combination of cross-project communities with project-specific knowledge practices for learning before, during and after, is a powerful combination for building a company-wide knowledge management system.

The details of how to set up and operate cross-project communities of practice are presented in Chapter 4.

Project review meetings

Every project has some form of regular project review meeting. The project leader and project team need to discuss progress, identify additional tasks and risks, and plan and set performance targets for the next phase activity. For example, the team might get together once a week to review progress in the previous week, to look at outstanding issues and actions, to look at new tasks and risks, to plan the work for the next week, and assign new actions to project team members.

The project review meetings should also include a review of learning. A good way to do this is to embed the AAR process as part of the project review meeting. The best place to introduce the AAR is in the early part of the meeting, when you are reviewing activity. So for example, a weekly project review meeting might follow the agenda below:

- a review of what was supposed to happen in the previous week;
- a review of what actually happened in the previous week;
- an analysis of the difference between the two, and derivation of lessons and actions;
- an updated status of where the project is at now;
- targets and plans for the coming week (in the context of a longer scale look-ahead);
- identification of new risks and opportunities;
- actions assigned;
- management of change.

Avoid holding the AAR component at the end of the meeting. It will usually be pushed off the agenda by discussions about activity, and the natural place for reviewing lessons is when you are reviewing performance. Learning should also be addressed prior to planning the next week's activity, so that the activity should be planned in the light of recent learning.

Knowledge engineers and managers

Although every project team member will be accountable for their own learning, and accountable for finding the knowledge they need in order to perform as best they can, there still need to be roles within the team accountable for the knowledge management system itself. The roles within the team may include some or all of the following.

The knowledge manager

The knowledge manager on a project team is the person responsible for making sure that:

- the team members access the knowledge they need to deliver the project;
- the team members identify and apply new knowledge in the project;
- the team members capture and share new knowledge created by the project;
- there is a documented system for managing the knowledge of the project team; and
- this system is adhered to during the life of the project.

The knowledge manager does not have to manage the knowledge themselves but they have to make sure that the knowledge is managed. That is their accountability: making sure that the knowledge is managed. This role within the project team is not necessarily a full-time role, nor is it necessarily a named role, but much as the project manager needs somebody to run the risk management system, and somebody to operate the project planning system, so they will need to somebody to look after the knowledge management system.

The knowledge manager needs to be a relatively senior person, with credibility. They need to be:

- a good listener, facilitator and communicator;
- au fait with the concepts of knowledge management;
- good at influencing;
- good at thinking strategically;
- experienced within the company, and within the business;
- well networked.

Knowledge engineers and learning historians

This may be the wrong choice of term, in which case you need to choose one that suits your own culture, but in a large project with a lot of learning, somebody may need to do the day-to-day facilitation of the knowledge activities. In BP, on the offshore oilrigs, this task is taken by a learning/technical limit coach who works within the project team to make sure that the technical limit/learning methodology is carried forward into day-to-day learning during operations. In the US Army, a small team of personnel ('operations officers') are assigned to any one major operation to carry out learning. This team is called a 'combined arms assessment team'.

In a major commercial project, where a considerable amount of new knowledge will be gained by the organisation, it may be necessary to appoint a full-time learning historian. This person's sole role is to capture the learning as the project progresses. At the end of the project they will produce a knowledge history. Obviously this is a significant investment in personnel, but where the project is the first of many, and the learning will have major applicability, then it may be worth investing in this resource. The learning historian will work within the knowledge management system, and will add learning to the system through interviewing people, recording what happens, taking photographs or video of crucial operations, and generally documenting what happens and what has been learned. For example, a construction organisation that is looking to expand into the Far East, might employ a learning historian on the first pilot project, so that the maximum knowledge can be gained from this for the benefit of all subsequent projects.

Knowledge engineers and learning historians should be experienced and credible people; not necessarily high in the hierarchy, but having several years of practical, hands-on experience. When young graduates were put in this role on the oil rigs, it was found that they didn't have the

Figure 3.4 Typical lessons and actions log

Date	Activity	Lesson	Action	Action owner	Due date	Open/ closed

credibility, nor the depth of understanding, to play the role. It was found better to use experienced blue-collar workers in the role instead.

Lessons and actions log

Any team that engages in learning during activity is going to generate a large number of lessons as they progress. Most of these lessons can be translated directly into actions (e.g. see the AAR example earlier), but they still need to be recorded somewhere. Somebody on the project (and this is almost certainly part of the role of the knowledge manager) needs to keep a lessons and actions log.

If the log is for the use only of the project team itself, this log need not be anything more sophisticated than a spreadsheet. The spreadsheet headings could be as shown in Figure 3.4. On the other hand, project teams could use an online lessons and actions log that can, at the end of the project, be automatically downloaded to the corporate lessons database. On any project with regular AARs, several hundred lessons may be recorded.

Learning after

Learning after the stages of the project involves:

- identifying new knowledge which has been learned by the project team;
- identifying all existing knowledge which has been reinforced or validated by the project team; and
- recording this knowledge of the sake of future projects.

'Learning after' processes should be applied whenever the team, or sub-team, have delivered their objectives (with interim objectives). The purpose of learning after is to make explicit, and capture, the know-how that has been gained. Most of this know-how is unconscious and tacit, and cannot be captured until it is discussed and made conscious. Also much of the know-how is shared between project members. In a multidisciplinary project, it is likely that no single member has a clear view on how things were achieved. Therefore learning must be discussed within the entire team, as a team process.

The old-school approach to project closeout all too often involved the project leader sitting down and writing his view of what the project delivered, and how that was achieved. In contrast, the learning after processes below involve the team sitting down and discussing what they have learned, and what lessons they would pass on to similar projects in future.

Retrospects

The retrospect is a robust, tried and tested approach for capturing lessons at the end of the project, a project stage, or sub-project. It was initially developed within BP in the early 1990s, but has spread to very many organisations now, in very many sectors and markets. Although it has some features in common with the AAR, it takes longer, it goes into greater depth, it makes sure that each individual on the team has a chance to contribute, and expresses the learning in terms of recommendations and advice for future projects.

Most organisations have some form of review after their major project activity. A post-project review, or appraisal, or audit, will generally look back at what happened in the project and look at what was achieved compared with the objectives. Was the project within the budget, over the budget, delivered to time, delivered to specification etc. A good appraisal or audit might go further than this, and look at the root causes behind things that went wrong, and may even look at the root causes behind things that went right. Sometimes the project leader alone writes this review, although more often it will involve the project team as well.

Where the retrospect differs from typical post-project appraisal, is that it goes beyond a historical review, and looks to the future, asking 'how do we avoid the problems in future projects?', 'How do we repeat the successes in future projects?', 'What can we give the next project team to help then deliver a perfect project?'

Retrospect set-up

It is important to schedule the retrospect at the end of the project or project phase, before the team disbands or moves on to fresh work, and before history becomes post-rationalised. Hold the retrospect while memories are fresh and while the project team is still available. It can be useful to combine the end-of-project retrospect with an end-of-project celebration, and treat it as a close-out exercise for the team. It is important that everybody on the team attends, and the client or customer for the project can be invited if appropriate.

Somebody who was not part of the project team should facilitate the retrospect. The better the facilitator, the better the outcome of the retrospect. Under no circumstances should the project team self-facilitate; they definitely need somebody external, who can help steer the process, ask the awkward questions, and make sure any undiscussables are discussed. Find a good facilitator who has a clear idea of the retrospect process, and of the purpose of the exercise. Retrospects are not complicated meetings, but they do need attention to purpose and attention to behaviours. Understanding, and following, the process is key to a successful outcome.

It is very powerful if you can find somebody who will re-use the knowledge – perhaps the project leader for the next similar project – and get them to attend the retrospect as an observer. Their presence will give the process a greater level of focus and legitimacy, and they can help make sure that the lessons which come out of the retrospects are expressed as useful recommendations and advice. For example, one organisation had just won a bid for major construction work in a former Soviet country. They invited the bid manager from a neighbouring country to attend their post-bid retrospect. As he was in the process of compiling a bid himself, much of the knowledge could be transferred immediately.

This knowledge re-user should not facilitate the retrospect; they will have their own agenda which should not be allowed to dominate the meeting, as they will not be the only users of this knowledge. The facilitator needs to make sure that all the knowledge from the project is captured, not just the knowledge that will be immediately re-used in the next project.

Retrospect process

The retrospect process is described below.

- *Introduction.* The first step in a retrospect is to set the scene by discussing the purpose of the meeting, the process of the meeting, and the ground rules for the meeting. Make it clear that the meeting is held to capture the learnings, in order to help future project teams. The purpose of the meeting is not to assign blame or to assign praise, but to make life easier for the next project team. Also make it clear what you will do with the output from the meeting, especially if you are recording the event. Once retrospects have become an established standard process, you don't really need to set the scene, but where this is a new process then you may need some careful set-up at the beginning of the meeting.

- *Project objectives.* Then you need to review the objectives of the project itself. Ask the project leader to start off this section. If they can find the original terms of reference, this is good because it adds some ground truth and reminds everybody of what they set out to do in the beginning. It is worth reviewing whether these objectives changed, whether there were any hidden objectives, and whether people had any personal objectives. Depending on the scale of the project, this may take between five minutes and 30 minutes to do this.

- *Project achievements.* The next stage involves looking at what actually happened in the project, and what was achieved at the end. Again, try and get to ground truth; what was the actual expenditure compared with the budget? What was the actual timing of the project compared with the plan? What feedback have they had from the client or customer, on the quality of the work? In a long or complicated project, you may need to draw a flow chart of what happened, before you can start to analyse it.

- *Analysis of successes.* The next stage begins the analysis. Start with what went well, and give everybody time to think through success factors and key positive steps in the process. Ask them to write down in front of them, three things that worked well.[2] Ask people in turn to identify their successes ('Fred – what worked well for you in this project? What was your greatest success factor?'); hold a group dialogue on each one to find the root causes of the success ('Everybody, why do you think this was successful? What did you do to ensure success?'); and continue the dialogue to ask how the success can be repeated in future ('So what would you recommend to a team doing this in future, to repeat the success? If you were doing it again tomorrow, what would you put in place?'). This section of the retrospect can take between 10 and 20 minutes for each person present (so if six people are present, it could take between one and two hours). Discussion may well stray into talking about the negatives as well; do not stifle discussion at this stage – let it run, until you have come up with the recommendations for next time. Then move onto the next person, and go back to the positives again. The purpose of this analysis is to come out with specific useful actionable recommendations for future projects, which will allow them to reproduce the identified success. During this process you may also identify procedures, documents, or other good practices which may be useful for future projects. For example, if a success factor was the clear definition of roles at the start of the project, then ask for a copy of the role definition document, which can then be re-used by future projects as a template, or as a starter for their own role definition document.

- *Analysis of disappointments.* Then you repeat the process, looking at things that 'could have gone better', analysing them through team dialogue to find how the root causes behind these disappointments or failures, and come to a team consensus on what future teams can do to avoid similar disappointments in future projects. If you are concerned that people might not openly discuss things that went wrong, start this section with the project leader (whom you have already asked to set the tone in being open). If they admit that things could have gone better, the rest of the team will open up too. Remember to always keep focused throughout this section on the advice for the future project teams.

- *Closure.* The mood of the meeting will have gone through several stages. People will have felt very positive reviewing the successes, and rather negative reviewing the disappointments. It is a good idea to end the retrospect with a 'closure' question, such as 'looking back, how satisfied are you with this project? Give it marks out of 10, where a ten means it went perfectly as far as I was concerned, zero means it was a total disaster, and five means it was entirely neutral'.

- *Offers for the next project.* If there is a clear follow-on project, or successor project, who will be looking to re-use the knowledge? A final step can be to ask the project team what they can provide to the next project to help them perform. Obviously they can give them the results of the retrospect, but they may be able to offer them documentation, advice, templates, plans, lists of contacts, and so on.

The key steps in the process are the two analysis steps. The role of the facilitator is to draw the discussion towards specific actionable advice and recommendations for future projects. Without firm facilitation, the meeting can easily degenerate into a discussion of what people liked about the project (or worse, into a blamestorming session). With firm facilitation, some very useful material can be developed for future teams.

Occasionally, when reviewing a difficult project, conflict may arise. Different people at the retrospect may have different perceptions of what happened to cause a breakdown or failure in the project. Arguments can start, tempers can rise. The way to turn conflict into a positive outcome is to ask the question 'what should we do *next time*, in future projects, to ensure this breakdown or failure does not happen again'. In many ways it does not matter precisely what happened this time, or whose fault it was, so long as everybody is agreed on how to do it better next time. In fact, the question 'what should we do next time' is the most powerful question to ask in retrospects. It is almost worth writing this question on a flip chart, and sticking it on the wall. The whole purpose of the retrospect is finding knowledge which can be reused next time, or in the next project.

Example retrospect content, from the end of a refinery maintenance project, is shown below. This content comes from the 'analysis of success factors' section, where one success factor from one of the participants is analysed by the group to derive recommendations for future projects. It is based on real content, but has been tidied up from the original transcripts.

> Facilitator: 'Mr X – what was the top success factor for you?'
>
> Mr X: 'One of the successes for me was the flexibility we had, so that when we hit problems in the project, we always had a back-up task we could go to.'
>
> Facilitator: 'How do you achieve that degree of flexibility?' (much discussion ensued, the conclusion being that) 'Detailed planning meant that everyone understood what was the next job to move on to if the current one was held up.'
>
> Facilitator: 'What should future projects do to achieve that degree of flexibility?'
>
> Group: 'Authority to change jobs should be pushed out to the individual team leaders. Also the team needs to hold a three-day look-ahead every day, so they know what jobs to move on to'.

This short discussion came up with two pieces of advice for future projects, which will enable them to reproduce the degree of flexibility that this project had. The whole retrospect might generate several dozen pieces of advice.

Retrospects for large or complex projects

It is difficult to hold a retrospect for more than about 15 people. Retrospects are based on a process of facilitated group dialogue, and it is hard to have dialogue if the group is too large. However, it is unusual that you would have so many people collaborating on shared objectives. In larger and more complex projects, they tend to be broken up into sub-projects, with smaller teams delivering sub-objectives.

For example, in the project shown in Figure 3.5, you would hold four retrospects. There will be one for each of the sub-projects, and then a fourth retrospect to review the coordination of the sub-projects. The sub-project teams should attend the retrospect for their sub-project, and the 'master project' retrospect will be attended by the project leader and the sub-project team leaders.

Retrospects and project stages

Retrospects are appropriate at the end of each project stage. However, the knowledge which will be captured will vary, depending on the project stage.

- A retrospect at the end of the scope/appraise stage will collect knowledge concerning project scoping and appraisal.

Figure 3.5 Sub-project structure

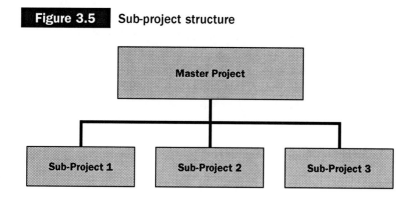

- A retrospect at the end of the concept select stage will collect knowledge concerning concept selection and ranking.
- A retrospect at the end of the design/define stage will collect knowledge concerning design and project definition.
- A retrospect at the end of the construct/execute stage will collect knowledge concerning the execution of the work and the construction of the deliverable.
- Each of these retrospects will also collect knowledge about the management and coordination of the project.

Recording retrospects

Knowledge has credibility when it is expressed by credible people – people with experience. Knowledge captured in the form of quotes or soundbites from the project team, can be seen as being the 'voice of experience'. If you are going to capture knowledge in this way, then the retrospect needs to be recorded carefully, recording people's own words as closely as possible, and recording who said what. You either have to take very detailed notes (speed-writing) or, if possible, you should audio-record the retrospect. Although people may worry about having a tape recorder present, you can reassure them that it is only for your own use, for transcription purposes, that any recordings will be destroyed after transcription, and that nothing will be published without giving the retrospect attendees the opportunity to edit it first. However, the amount of knowledge that comes out during a retrospect is so huge, that often audio-recording is the only practical way to capture it all.

It can also be useful to summarise some of the key retrospect lessons on video. At the end of the retrospect, when the lessons have been identified and discussed, ask a few of the more eloquent speakers to summarise what has been learned, and what they would recommend to future projects based on that learning. These small video summaries can be a good and engaging way of recording some of the key lessons.

Chapter 4 discusses how the knowledge which comes out of retrospects can be packed for transfer between projects.

Knowledge histories

Sometimes a project is too large, too dispersed, or contains people who are so busy and unavailable, that it is impossible to schedule an end-of-project retrospect with everyone in the one room at the same time. An alternative approach, the *knowledge history*, collects knowledge through a compilation of one-on-one interviews with project team members. For example, a manufacturer and retailer of branded products went through a major mergers and acquisitions programme, which was conducted by a fairly small team of very high ranking staff. It proved impossible to bring the team together for a retrospect, so a knowledge history was conducted. Each of the high-ranking team members was interviewed individually, and the lessons were collated into a single document.

The scale of the knowledge history is entirely dependent on the number of people you need to interview, and the larger the project team you interview, the more working days you need to allow for the process. A good rule of thumb is to allow between 1.5–2 working days for each person interviewed. So a knowledge history based on interviews with ten people will take between 15 and 20 working days to collect, edit and complete.

Given the resource required to undertake a knowledge history, they will only be applied to the most important and strategic projects.

Knowledge history process

The process of the knowledge history is based on interviewing. The analysis, collation and distillation of the results is also a very large part of the process. If the scale of the knowledge history is a large one, you may need a team of interviewers and analysts. A knowledge history from a project with a 10-person project team can be done on your own; from a project with more than 20 in the extended team you might need some assistance.

The process is as follows:

- *Set the expectation.* This is going to be a big effort. Make sure you have prominent sponsorship from the project customer and project leader.

- *Identify the people to interview.* These need to be key players who had 'skin in the game'. The project leader, the main client, the core project team, and key sub-project team members should all be interviewed.

- *Put together a group of people to conduct the knowledge history.* They will need journalist skills, interviewing skills, analysis skills and writing skills.

- *Conduct the interviews.* These need to be free-flowing open interviews, not 'market research' questionnaires. They need to be focused on drawing out the learning. This sort of interviewing is a skill, which can be learned, but you cannot assume that people can do it without training. The interviews need to be recorded and transcribed.

- *Transcribe the interviews.* Select the quotes you will use from the interviews, and check these with the interviewees.

- *Analyse the results.* Identify the common themes, and distil out the lessons. This can be a huge job – in a big exercise, you can spend several days on this step.

- *Package the knowledge history.* Packaging knowledge is discussed below in Chapter 4.

- *Feed back the results.* If you can, then get the interviewees together in groups, starting with the sponsor group, and discuss the results of the history with them, reflect on it together, and talk through its implications. The knowledge asset can be updated with these new insights, before the next workshop.

- *Roll out* the packaged knowledge to identified customers, the community of practice, and the entire organisation.

As an example, a knowledge history was conducted in BP Turkey in 2002, on the topic of road safety. Through a long programme of culture change, BP Turkey had been able to reduce its road traffic fatality and injury rate by a staggering amount. In order to help other parts of the group to replicate this success, BP Turkey commissioned a knowledge history to capture the know-how about improving road safety. Twenty-seven people were interviewed in Turkey, and the interviews were transcribed and compiled into a knowledge asset. As of June 2005, this was accessible at *http://www.roadsafetyturkey.com/*.

Knowledge management in multi-company projects

Many large construction projects use an alliance or partnership of many companies, contractors and sub-contractors to deliver the project. This adds a degree of complexity to knowledge management; technical, terminological and cultural complexity. Some of the issues which need to be addressed are as follows.

- *Cultural alignment.* Knowledge management is new to many organisations, and there will need to be a degree of discussion and alignment before all parties are likely to agree to apply a project knowledge management system. Senior managers in the various companies may need to be brought on board, in order to give the go-ahead to their staff. Of course it is advisable to stipulate in the pre-tendering and in the contract that all parties will be involved in the knowledge management system, but you need more than compliance, you need engagement. So, some workshops will be needed to discuss the knowledge management system, and to ensure buy-in. Many of the processes described in this chapter (peer assists, customer interviews, AARs, retrospects) will help towards alignment anyway, as they promote open dialogue and discussion.

- *Clarity on terminology.* Different companies use different names for the same things. You need to clarify the terminology up front. One company's jargon is often different from another's, even if they are partners in the same project. You can't share knowledge if you don't use the same words.

- *Clarity on roles and responsibilities.* As far as roles and responsibilities for the knowledge management system are concerned, these need to be clearly defined in any knowledge management plan for the project (see Chapter 5).

- *Co-location.* There is no doubt that co-location of the multi-company core team radically improves communication and knowledge sharing.

- *Consistent technology.* However you plan to capture, store and share knowledge, you need to use technology to which everyone has access. You may even need to go to the length of setting up an extranet, purely for storing and sharing knowledge, information and data for the project.

- *Knowledge ownership.* You need to get clear on who owns, and who will be entitled to use, the knowledge that is created by the project. Ideally, all parties should co-own the knowledge, subject to confidentiality agreements. This will give them far more of an incentive to contribute freely.

Notes

1. It is common to talk of people going 'up' the learning curve. However when drawing learning curves for cost or time performance (particularly in the oil industry), these are generally shown as coming 'down' (i.e. costs reduce over time). It is left to the reader to translate these expressions into their own business context.
2. The purpose of asking them to write down the item is first to force some individual reflection, and second to avoid people 'shifting' their item to fit in with others'.

The flow of knowledge between projects

Chapter 3 was concerned with the flow of knowledge within a single project, and discussed knowledge entering the project at various stages (through 'learning before' activities), knowledge being identified and applied within the project (through 'learning during' activities), and knowledge being captured at various stages for future use (through 'learning after' activities).

This chapter deals with the flow of knowledge between projects, and looks at how the 'learning after' for one project can become the 'learning before' for another.

Figure 4.1 (as discussed in Chapter 1) shows some of the issues that need to be addressed in any knowledge management system. Although knowledge will largely be collected by the projects, and accessed by the projects, there needs to be a larger system that can collate and organise knowledge from many projects. Some of the questions that need to be answered with regard to this cross-project system are as follows.

- Who owns and administers the system of exchanging knowledge between projects?
- Who has the authority to say whether one piece of knowledge is more valid than another?
- Where will this knowledge be stored?
- What process do you need for purging the system of old, out-of-date, or invalid knowledge?
- What you do about the knowledge that cannot be written down; the uncodifiable knowledge?
- How do you prompt future projects to use this knowledge?
- What is the process for updating company standards and policies in the light of new knowledge?

Figure 4.1   The 12-component knowledge management framework

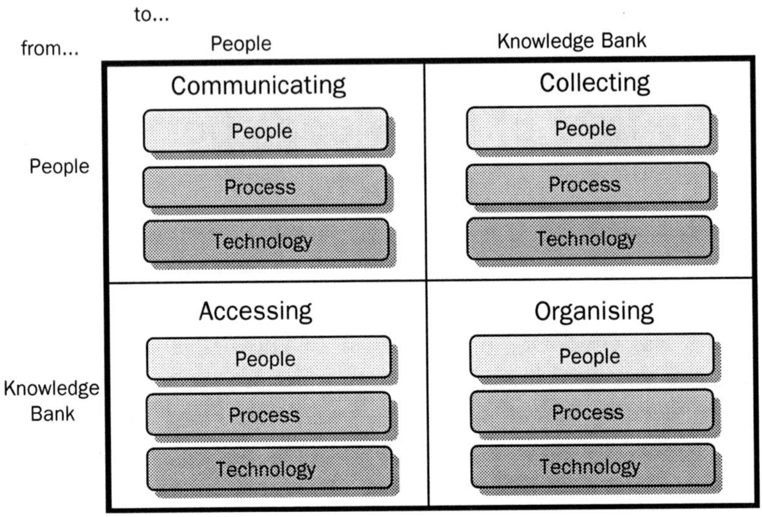

Ownership of cross-project knowledge

The first question to answer concerns the ownership of the cross-project knowledge. You need to decide who has accountability for making sure the knowledge is shared between projects, and who has accountability for looking after that knowledge; for storing it, organising it, validating it, distilling it, keeping it fresh and live, and weeding out the old out-of-date knowledge.

Ownership of cross-project knowledge

In any one company, there are three possible approaches to assigning accountability for cross-project knowledge sharing.

- The accountability for cross-project knowledge sharing is centralised within a 'projects best practice' group within the organisation. Serco, for example, centralises its project knowledge in the Serco best practice centre.

- The accountability of cross-project knowledge sharing is decentralised to the communities of practice. Each community will take accountability for its own discipline. So, for example, the project managers community will look after project management learning, the engineering community will look after engineering learning, the procurement community will look after procurement learning. Each community will appoint subject matter experts to manage specific knowledge areas. This model is largely applied within BP Major Projects.

- The accountability for cross-project knowledge sharing is decentralised to discipline-specific centres of excellence (or even to single experts). So, for example, project management learning may be the remit of a project managers centre of excellence, engineering learning will be handled by engineering technology group, and a procurement function will look after procurement learning.

Whichever model you choose, the accountable body needs to have the authority to validate knowledge – to say 'this knowledge is valid best practice, this other knowledge is not best practice'. The organisational hierarchy needs to recognise this authority, and so does the community of users. So, the communities need to be involved in every model. They either need to do the validating, or approve the people who do the validating. Often validation is done by people who are recognised experts, who can be trusted to speak for the company, and speak for the community.

If you centralise knowledge transfer within a 'projects best practice' group, this group also needs to involve and coordinate the communities of practice.

If knowledge sharing is decentralised to the communities of practice, then the communities need to appoint subject matter experts, or recognised technical authorities, who can validate knowledge.

Ownership in multi-company projects

Cross-project knowledge sharing is more of an issue in projects where more than one company is involved. If the companies form a semi-permanent alliance, such as the BP/Bovis Alliance, then the alliance itself can look after knowledge sharing, using one of the models described above. If the alliance is not permanent (for example BP and Siemens may collaborate on a project this year, and next year BP could be working with Amec, and Siemens with Shell) – who then will coordinate cross-project knowledge sharing?

Certainly each company should develop their own system for cross-project knowledge sharing. In the example above, BP will have their own internal system, so will Shell, so will Amec, so will Siemens. This approach of separate knowledge management systems is possibly the only approach that will work successfully for knowledge which the organisations recognise to be of competitive advantage. There are very few companies that will risk sharing key competitive knowledge, even accidentally, with their competitors.

There are also organisations for cross-project knowledge sharing, often set up through industry or government initiatives. An example from the UK would be the 'Constructing Excellence' initiative, run by the Chartered Institute of Building, which seeks to identify and share best practices in the construction industry. Any project should subscribe to such initiatives, but should also make full use of any in-house cross-project knowledge sharing system.

Transfer of explicit knowledge between projects

Chapter 3 discussed the processes and accountable roles for capturing knowledge during project activity. The knowledge manager (sometimes helped by knowledge engineers) will make sure that the project team holds after action reviews, retrospects and sometimes learning histories. These activities will identify, make explicit, and capture lessons learned[1] from the project, and store them in some sort of knowledge store or database (which ideally will be a cross-project database). However, Figure 4.2 shows that this is only the first step in a cycle of knowledge re-use.

Once lessons learned have been captured from many projects, the next step is to derive best practices. This derivation is done by a cross-project body as described above – a community of practice, a group of subject-matter experts, a project centre, or whatever model fits best within your organisation. This body will compare the lessons, look at the ones that come up most frequently, decide which lessons can be recommended as good practices, decide which lessons are one-offs of limited applicability, remove the duplicates, resolve the contradictions, and develop best practices.[2]

If best practices are sufficiently well validated through use, the company may adopt them as a mandatory approach such as a company

Figure 4.2 The knowledge re-use cycle

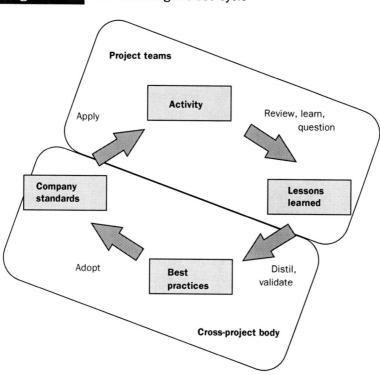

standard.[3] Again, it will be the responsibility of the central body to decide which best practices should be adopted as company standard.

Once practices are adopted as company standard, they should (if all is well) be automatically applied in future projects. Ideally, future projects will also use company best practices as a recommended approach, and they will also look through the lessons learned database to search for more knowledge. The combination of embedding knowledge into company standards, and providing knowledge as best practices and lessons learned, allows future projects to start from a full level of knowledge.

This cycle is one of knowledge maturation. It is fed by knowledge processes within the projects, and if these processes are held regularly then there will be a regular feed of knowledge into the cycle. It is up to the central body to decide what frequency of update to the best practices is needed, and therefore how rapidly the cycle needs to turn. The US Army claims that under combat conditions a lesson from an active unit can be turned into Army Doctrine (their term for organisational standards) within 48 hours. Many commercial organisations would struggle to do this within 48 weeks! The organisation needs to ask themselves 'how rapidly do we need to learn?' and put in place a system for moving lessons through the cycle at the required speed.

The steps of capturing knowledge, and of applying knowledge, are the responsibility of the project teams. The steps of distilling knowledge into best practices, and then validating and adopting these as company standards, are the responsibility of the central cross-project body. This section looks at those steps in more detail.

Storing lessons learned

If lessons are being learned from many projects, sourced from retrospects and AARs, then these lessons need to be captured and stored somewhere where they can be compared and transferred from one project to another. They need to be captured in a consistent format, and stored in a central system. This is likely to be some sort of lessons learned database to which all the projects will have access.

Lessons learned databases are common components of a company-wide knowledge management system, and many examples of such databases can be found on the World Wide Web. Unfortunately, they can often be an extremely poor way of transferring knowledge, and commonly suffer from bad structure and/or unhelpful content. If you intend to put together a lessons learned database, the advice below will help you produce something that can help deliver sustainable business performance improvement.

Lessons learned databases

The lessons within the database should be phrased as advice for subsequent projects. People will look in the database because they are looking for guidance. They have some activity planned, or under way, and they are looking to avoid mistakes and repeat successes. They want to know what they should do, and they are looking for ideas, recommendations or advice. What they unfortunately often find is history or anecdote. If a lesson is to be valuable, it should give the reader some insight of how they should approach similar problems. In other words, the lessons should transfer know-how. In addition, the advice should be specific, and actionable. Examples follow of good and bad lessons taken at random from an online lessons learned database.

> Periodic inspection and preventive maintenance on cranes are important to ensure safe operation. (This is certainly true, but is more of a truism than a lesson. How periodic should investigation be? What sort of preventative maintenance? More details are needed)

> A suspect grade 8 bolt was found in a load binder on a gas cylinder pallet purchased on a P-Card. (This is not really a lesson. What should the reader do about this? What is the advice?)

> Exothermic Reaction During Tank Foaming. As the top of an enclosed structure such as a tank is neared, lower-volume nozzles and extra caution should be used to compensate for lack of visibility, which can lead to uneven application of foam and unwanted exothermic reaction. As a good practice, free liquids in tanks should be sampled and an informed engineering judgment should be made regarding how to deal with them before proceeding with foaming operations. In addition, as a good practice, the Procurement Buyer should be notified on occurrences when subcontractors are involved. (A good example, containing actionable advice about sampling and procurement, though some rules of thumb about interpreting the samples would be even more helpful)

Lessons, to be useful, need to be actionable, specific, and addressed as forward-looking advice. Poor lessons are worse than useless, as they clog up the database and deter people from looking for the good lessons. Some quality control mechanism is needed, before lessons are released to the public domain, to ensure lesson quality. For example, the BP Well Engineering lessons database has two levels of lesson: unvalidated and validated. A lesson needs to be checked by a senior drilling engineer before it is given 'validated' status, at which point the lesson can be forwarded to other teams.

Database structure

The database should be structured according to the needs of the 'knowledge user' (see Chapter 1). People who come to access lessons from the database should be able to find what they are looking for very easily. If they don't find relevant and useful knowledge within a few minutes, they will leave and never come back. Think about the needs and interests of the knowledge user, think about how the knowledge will be re-used, and think about how you should structure the database to give them access to what they need most easily. A common mistake is to structure the database according to how the knowledge was supplied. The lessons might be grouped by project name, for example, or by year of completion of the projects. Neither of these attributes is of particular interest to the knowledge user. They are more likely to want to find all the lessons on procuring steel pipe, safety while working at height, or partnering with a particular national authority; in other words, lessons concerning the particular issue that they face.

Compare Figures 4.3 and 4.4, which show the structure of an imaginary example lessons learned database, and ask yourself which of the two would be more useful to someone in a future project looking for advice on (for example) contracting during the concept design stage?

Figure 4.3 Helpful lessons database structure

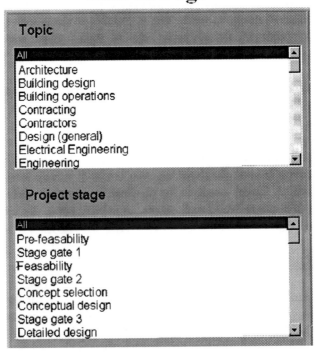

In addition, it goes without saying that the database should be searchable. Search should be possible on many fields, as well as a free text search. Ideally the free text search should be semi-intelligent. For example, in a global organisation a search for 'vapour detection systems' should also return items about 'vapor detection systems'.

Ease of entry

The criteria above (a user-friendly structure, user-friendly content, and the ability to search) are the most important success criteria for a lessons learned database. Once these have been satisfied, then you then can start to think about criteria such as the ease of data entry. Make sure you prompt the person who is entering the data to think hard about what advice they want to give to the knowledge user, and to think hard about how they should categorise the lesson so that it can be found most easily. After that, data entry should be largely a question of selecting options and filling in boxes.

Figure 4.4　Less helpful lessons database structure

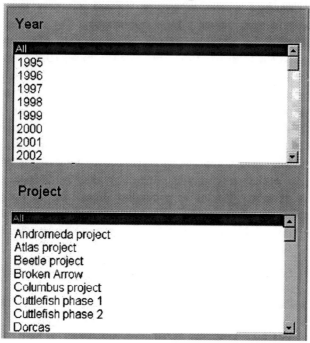

Keep the name with the knowledge

Individuals are motivated to share knowledge in a number of ways. They may be motivated by a desire to help others, by pride in their own successes, or by a desire to demonstrate good knowledge-sharing behaviours. In each case, this motivation is reinforced if their name goes with the lesson. So, it is not just 'A lesson on improving heat exchanger efficiency', it is 'Bill Paterson's lesson on improving heat exchanger efficiency'. Bill Paterson therefore gets some credit and his profile raised. If you remove his name from the lesson, then he can easily feel that 'his' knowledge is being taken from him and passed off as someone else's knowledge. In addition, it is very unlikely that Bill will be able to store in the database all the knowledge that needs to be exchanged about improving heat exchanger efficiency, and the knowledge user will sooner or later want to pick up the telephone and speak with Bill. So, make sure the name goes with the knowledge, and that the telephone number and e-mail address go with the name.

Use pictures

In transferring knowledge, as in so many other applications, a picture is worth a thousand words. A lessons learned database that transfers lessons only in text, misses a huge opportunity. The originator of the lessons should be able to attach photographs, diagrams, audio recordings, video files; whatever they need in order to demonstrate the lesson. For example, in offshore operations nowadays, the drilling crew will frequently keep a digital camera handy, and photograph equipment before and after it is used. Whether operations go well or badly, the photographic record can often be very valuable in transferring knowledge to other teams. In a construction setting, it may be very useful to have photographs taken during construction, or it might be useful to be able to attach engineering drawings to the lessons database. Databases of safety lessons in particular should be set up to handle photographs, as photographs of accidents and near misses can be extremely powerful ways of alerting others about danger and risk.

Build in a 'push' facility

One of the biggest hurdles in any knowledge management system is getting people to look for knowledge, advice and lessons. No matter how well structured and searchable the lessons learned database may be, this will not help if people don't go to the database in the first place. However, it may be possible to set up a 'push database' which will forward lessons to interested parties, rather than requiring them to go and search.

An example of this is the LINK database within BP. This is a form-based database for lessons from drilling oil wells. At the end of a well, the project team will hold a retrospect, and they will identify lessons to go into LINK. These lessons take about 10–15 minutes each to enter, and have to go through a quality-control process before they become public. The lessons are categorised according to the type of well (deep water wells, onshore wells, wells drilled from production platforms etc), the type of operation (surveying, cementing, completing etc), and the value of the lessons (how much it cost to fix the problem, or how much time was saved). There are about 50 wells teams around the BP group, and each team nominates a contact person to work with LINK. This person subscribed to LINK on behalf of the team, registers the types of knowledge that their team is interested in, and any time a corresponding lesson is entered into LINK, anywhere in the world, it is immediately forwarded to this nominated person. For example, a wells team in Trinidad might be interested in high-pressure, deep water wells, so all lessons from anywhere in the world about high-pressure deep water wells will be automatically e-mailed to the LINK contact person for Trinidad. This person can look at the lesson, and see if it is worth following up.

This 'push' capability adds tremendous value to a lessons learned database. However, this example also shows that for the LINK technology to work, it needs to be combined with a process for identifying and capturing knowledge (the end-of-well retrospect), with accountable roles for entering and receiving knowledge (the LINK administrator), and with the culture of openness to receiving knowledge from other teams. All of the components of people, process, technology and culture (the critical elements in Figure 1.4) are addressed, as shown in Figure 4.5.

Best practices and knowledge assets

No matter how good a lessons learned database you have, it will not be in itself a complete knowledge management solution. If you are successful in populating the database with lessons, then it will rapidly become too cumbersome to wade through in search of knowledge. For example, when the database contains two or three lessons to do with contract strategy in Angola, it is useful. When it contains two hundred lessons (some of which may contradict each other, some of which may

Figure 4.5 Elements of the knowledge management system for BP Well projects

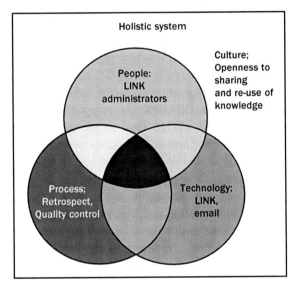

repeat each other, some of which may be several years out of date) it is less useful, and it is time to build a best practice[4] for Angola contracting strategy. This best practice document will collate the sum total of existing lessons, remove the duplicates and out-of-date lessons, resolve any discrepancies and contradictions, and package the remaining knowledge into a form which is tailored for the needs of the knowledge user.

The degree of care you need to put into packaging the best practice document depends on the context in which it will be reused. Nancy Dixon, in her book *Common Knowledge*, differentiates between 'near transfer' and 'far transfer'.

- Near Transfer is involved when knowledge will be used in a very similar context from that in which it originated. For example, best practices for changing the engine of a Mini Cooper, or for constructing a K10000 tower crane, will be an example of Near Transfer, as all Mini Coopers have the same sort of engine, and all K10000 tower cranes are alike. Near Transfer does not need too much background explanation; a series of instructions and diagrams may be all you need.

- Far Transfer is involved when knowledge will be used in a different context from that in which it originated. For example, best practices in opening a new head office in a foreign country will be an example of Far Transfer, as each foreign country will bring with it a different context, even though the issues will be mostly similar. Far Transfer needs a lot of explanation, a lot of background, and also links to people who can put the knowledge into context.

Best practices for 'near transfer'

A classic example of best practices that have been packaged for near transfer, is a cookery book. Cookery books contain abundant know-how. They enable you to know how to bake a cake, cook a casserole, or create a four-course dinner for guests. The way in which the knowledge is presented in a cookery book can be taken as a model for presenting knowledge in a near transfer best practice document.

- The cookery book tells you precisely what you need. It gives you the exact ingredients, the exact quantities, and details of the equipment you will need.

- It gives clear and concise instructions about what to do and how to proceed, and it presents these according to the sequence of operations.

- It gives tips and hints about how to maximise performance.

- It often gives a photograph of the finished product, to give you some idea of what you are aiming for.

Best practice documents for near transfer can be organised in a similar way. The document should tell you what to do, when to do it, how to do it, and what the outcome should look like. It should be structured in such a way as to be most easy to follow for the user. The knowledge can be presented as instructions, or as checklists, or as frequently asked questions. The US Army Center for Army Lessons Learned present their best practice documents as illustrated instructional documents, to walk you through the techniques. One legal group presents their best practice documents as annotated examples of the current 'best-in-class' example of a confidentiality agreement, or contract agreement, and so on. The exact format you choose for the document will vary from one company to another, and from one community to another. Whichever format you choose, however, it should tell the reader what to do, how to do it, and what the end result should be like.

It should also tell the reader who to contact for more details. The best practice document will also need an author or validator, who needs to be a recognised authority – someone who can speak for the community and claim that 'this practice is a best practice'. There should be a feedback mechanism, such as an e-mail address or phone number, so that anyone who finds an improvement to the practice, or who finds a better practice, can contact the author and offer their new knowledge.

Knowledge assets for 'far transfer'

Far transfer is rather more complex than teaching someone how to bake a cake or cook a casserole. Because the knowledge may be used in a different context from that in which it originated, you can't package the knowledge as a set of instructions. For example, you might learn about the issues of moving offices from a series of office moves, but the next move may be in a different city or a different country, and it will be impossible to put together a 'recipe' for office moves.

Knowledge packaged for far transfer is more liable to be in the form of stories, advice, guidance, and recommendations. Knowledge packaged in this way is referred to in BP, De Beers and many other large organisations as a *knowledge asset*, and a knowledge asset will contain the following components:

- *Context*. All knowledge lives within a context. For example, the advice given in a knowledge asset about opening new offices will vary depending on whether the context is that new offices should be prestige buildings, or should be as cheap as possible.

- *Advice*. This forms the high-value content of the knowledge asset. The advice and recommendations should be presented wherever possible in the words of the project team members, and illustrated with stories and anecdotes. Direct quotes will give credibility to the advice, while the stories, anecdotes and explanations will give context to the advice. In addition, if you identify the people who you are quoting, then the reader of the knowledge asset knows who to contact for more detail. Figure 4.6 shows an example extract from a knowledge asset; a knowledge asset created on 'How to implement knowledge management'. The knowledge is presented in FAQ (frequently asked questions) format, with the answers to the questions illustrated by quotes from the knowledge management project team. Figure 4.6 shows part of one section of the knowledge asset, where one question

Figure 4.6 Extract from the BP knowledge asset created from a retrospect at the end of knowledge management implementation

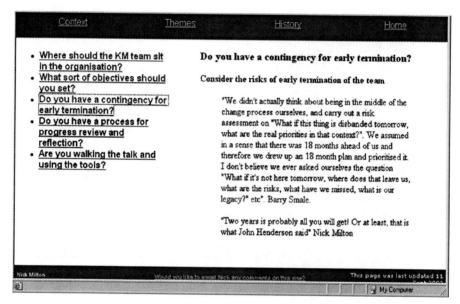

('Do you have a communications strategy') is answered, with the answers set in context of the team members' own experience.

- *Stories and case histories.* When attempting far transfer of knowledge, the knowledge user needs to understand the advice in the context in which it was created, before they can recontextualise it into their own context. This means that they have to know the background story to what happened. Include case histories and stories from the projects that provided the knowledge, to give the reader as much background as possible.

- *Video.* It can be powerful to present some or all of these stories in video format (see Figure 4.7). Some people prefer to learn through listening and seeing, rather than through reading text. In addition, stories in video form capture some of the personality and passion of the people speaking.

- *Links to people.* You can never capture all the knowledge and experience in text form. Sooner or later, the reader will need to find one of the original project team and ask for more details, or find one of the company experts. Knowledge assets should contain contact

Figure 4.7 Stories, recorded in video form, from a knowledge asset about knowledge management implementation at De Beers

details for the knowledgeable and experienced people who can provide more context and more detailed advice.

- *Links to documents.* The reader will also find it valuable to see example documents, example project plans, example contracts and so on, which will give them something to base their own documents on (Figure 4.8). This will be particularly valuable if the documents are annotated, so the reader can see which components are recommended practices. For example, a contract could be annotated to demonstrate (with the benefit of hindsight) the clauses which were vital, as opposed to the clauses which caused trouble.

- *Metadata.* The knowledge asset needs an owner, a creation date, and some explanation of what it is for, and how it was put together.

- *Consider readability.* Make sure the knowledge asset can be read by the colour-blind, or the partially sighted. Your organisation may have some guidelines on publication and access.

Figure 4.8 Document library from a knowledge asset (the BP knowledge asset on refinery shutdowns and turnarounds)

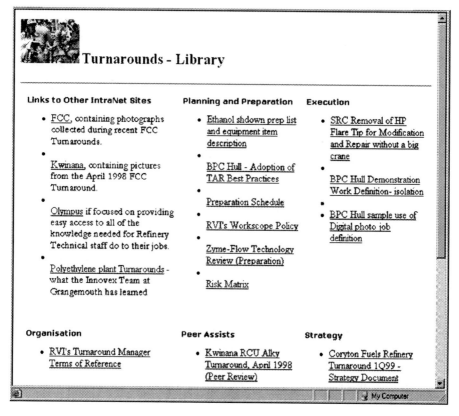

Turnarounds - Library

Links to Other IntraNet Sites

- FCC, containing photographs collected during recent FCC Turnarounds.

- Kwinana, containing pictures from the April 1998 FCC Turnaround.

- Olympus if focused on providing easy access to all of the knowledge needed for Refinery Technical staff do to their jobs.

- Polyethylene plant Turnarounds - what the Innovex Team at Grangemouth has learned

Planning and Preparation

- Ethanol shdown prep list and equipment item description

- BPC Hull - Adoption of TAR Best Practices

- Preparation Schedule

- RVI's Workscope Policy

- Zyme-Flow Technology Review (Preparation)

- Risk Matrix

Execution

- SRC Removal of HP Flare Tip for Modification and Repair without a big crane

- BPC Hull Demonstration Work Definition- isolation

- BPC Hull sample use of Digital photo job definition

Organisation

- RVI's Turnaround Manager Terms of Reference

Peer Assists

- Kwinana RCU Alky Turnaround, April 1998 (Peer Review)

Strategy

- Coryton Fuels Refinery Turnaround 1Q99 - Strategy Document

Company standards and procedures

Knowledge that has been proven repeatedly in practice, can become embedded in company standards and procedures. It moves beyond 'best practice' to become 'established practice', or 'required practice'. There needs to be official endorsement of this move, by the owner of the company standards. Ideally the company standards should be owned by the same person who owns the best practice, namely the company subject matter experts. Often, however, the standards are owned at a high level, with the company experts acting as advisors. So, the chief engineer may 'own' the company engineering standards, though much of the actual work of deriving and updating practices and standards will, for example, be delegated to an engineering materials subject matter expert, a rotating equipment subject matter expert, an instrumentation and control systems subject matter expert, and so on. The role of these experts is described below.

Maintaining and updating standards and best practices

The ideal situation is one where the company standards always reflect current best practice, and are applied by all projects as a springboard for further innovations where required. The standard becomes a starting point, rather than an absolute. This situation requires continuous learning, and also a continuous desire for continuous improvement. Any new advances are captured instantly, assessed, and fed straight into an update of the standards. The learning loop shown in Figure 4.2 therefore is in continuous operation, and whoever is involved in maintaining the standards needs to be actively involved in this loop.

The company needs to determine the correct frequency for updating standards and best practices, and needs to determine the process by which updates are validated. In Shell, for example, company standards are reviewed and updated on an annual basis. In BP Engineering, the update frequency is every two years. By contrast, the US Army (as quoted above) can update standards within 48 hours if necessary. Each organisation needs to determine the update frequency that suits their particular rate of learning. When engaged in new activities, where conditions are changing rapidly, then best practices and standards need to be updated frequently. For example, knowledge is advancing rapidly in subsea engineering technology, and any standards and best practices in this field may need to be updated every few months. If standards and best practice start to lag behind current practice, than they become discredited and people may start to ignore them. On the other hand, standards and best practices in the field of recruitment, procurement or contracts may change more slowly, and an annual or biannual update may be sufficient.

New lessons coming from the projects are used to update the standards and best practices, and the person responsible for this update will take lessons from the lessons learned database. As the standards are updated, the database should also be updated, and any old lessons, contradictory lessons, or low-value lessons can be cleaned out. This housekeeping exercise also maintains the credibility of the stored knowledge by clearing out the junk.

Any updates to standards and best practices need some sort of endorsement and validation. Any best practice needs to be endorsed as being 'best', and any standards need to be seen as a valid standard approach. The user community within the projects needs to feel they can trust this endorsement and validation step. If, for example, all the validation is done by a remote team in head office that nobody knows, then the project teams may be reluctant to use the standards and practices, because they don't know whether they can trust them. The validation and endorsement needs to be done by respected and trusted experts, or (even better) through involvement of the community of practice. The more the community feels they are involved in the validation process, the more they feel they can trust the outcome, and the more likely they will be to apply the best practices and standards.

Broadcasting new standards and best practices

Every time there is an update to the standards, or a new best practice has been developed, it needs to be communicated to the organisation. This could be done through an e-mail drop, an announcement to the community, or through regular newsletters. Whichever communication works best, is the one needs to be applied. For example, BP Drilling use a regular community newsletter, *Well Connected*, to broadcast many of the new technologies and best practices. This newsletter has a very wide circulation, and is read by most of the members of the community.

The role of the subject matter experts

The subject matter experts play a key role in managing and organising the explicit knowledge of an organisation. They are the long-term stewards of the knowledge, as it is exchanged between projects. Each subject matter expert will be responsible for one area of knowledge and expertise. They will be responsible for keeping the collected knowledge up-to-date and validated, and for broadcasting new knowledge back to the organisation. They will also maintain best practices and corporate standards within this specific area of knowledge.

Some of their specific responsibilities include the following:

- monitoring the development of knowledge within their specific area of expertise;

- ensuring that knowledge is collected and shared from significant pieces of work;
- promoting peer assists and personal connections between the projects;
- developing and publicising best practices in the subject matter;
- developing, and agreeing with management, corporate standards in the subject matter;
- updating best practices and standards in the subject matter as required;
- ensuring that the best practices and standards are made available to all users;
- publicising and rolling out new knowledge, and updated best practices and standards;
- monitoring use of any relevant knowledge asset, and acting on feedback to improve this;
- liaising with any network coordinator in the subject matter;
- ensuring all reference material is kept available, accessible, high quality and up-to-date;
- monitoring the organisational performance in the subject matter.

The subject matter expert needs to be a senior and highly respected practitioner in the subject matter, and a confident communicator in many media. They need to play a key role in any relevant communities of practice, and sometimes the community coordinator and the subject matter expert are the same person. It certainly helps if they have a reasonable awareness of the theory and practice of knowledge management, and of the knowledge management tools and processes used in the organisation.

Transfer of tacit knowledge between projects

Not all project knowledge will be captured in lessons learned, and much of the knowledge will remain in the heads of the project team members. This is especially true of the less codifiable knowledge. If the project knowledge managers have done their job well, and held AARs and retrospects at the critical points, then as much knowledge as possible will have been collected and codified, but a significant amount will still remain in people's heads as tacit knowledge. The system for transferring cross-project knowledge needs to address tacit knowledge, and its transfer from person to person, as well as explicit captured knowledge. The traditional approach to tacit knowledge transfer is to transfer the people who hold the knowledge. So, projects would be staffed by people with specific expertise and knowledge, and if you need knowledge, you hire a knowledgable person. However, there are methods of spreading knowledge more widely, such as peer assists (Chapter 3) and communities of practice. These methods are described below.

Staff transfer

The traditional approach for bringing knowledge into the project, by staffing the project team with experienced people, is still an important component of knowledge management for projects. Each project member will bring in their own knowledge and experience from the other projects that they have worked on, and collectively they can pool this knowledge and apply it to the new project. Certainly, a crucial project should look around for the people with the most relevant experience from previous projects, and should sign them up to the project team. However, this approach, if used as the only mechanism for accessing tacit knowledge, has limitations. Each team member only has access to their own personal knowledge and experience, and each team member can only be on one project at a time. There is therefore no mechanism for accessing all the tacit knowledge from all the previous and current projects. Staff transfer needs to be supported by other mechanisms, such as peer assists and communities of practice, as described below.

Peer assists

Peer assists are an extremely powerful mechanism for sharing knowledge between projects. These knowledge-sharing meetings have already been described in detail in Chapter 3. In a large company, peer assists should be a mandatory component of major projects, before the concept selection and design stages, in order to maximise the input of cross-project ideas and experience in the early stages.

Communities of practice

Communities of practice have already been introduced in Chapter 3 as a mechanism for projects to access knowledge during project activity, from their peers around the world. Communities of practice are peer networks of practitioners within an organisation, who share knowledge with each other to help solve problems and improve performance. Communities of practice should be set up for all the major professional disciplines within the organisation. For example, you might need a marketing community, an engineering community, a procurement community, and a project managers community. For a community of practice to operate effectively, it needs to be given the following enablers:

- an identity
- an energetic coordinator
- subject matter experts (or other designated owners of community knowledge)
- a launch meeting
- critical mass
- a way to ask questions and give answers
- a way to find each other
- a place to store common property (common knowledge)
- terms of reference
- a social network
- face-to-face meetings
- a level of autonomy
- a management sponsor

A company which plans to use communities of practice as a cross-project knowledge sharing mechanism needs to consider all of the above. Some of these crucial aspects are discussed in more detail below.

Community identity

Members of a community are happy to share knowledge with each other because they feel a sense of identity with each other. They see each other as fellow practitioners, sharing the same challenges, facing the same issues, and having valuable knowledge to share. People will feel 'at home' in a community if they identify with the community topic and with the community members. Therefore the most effective communities tend to be the ones that deal with people's core jobs. In Shell, some of the most effective communities are the communities of geologists and geophysicists; people with a specialist discipline, who work full-time in the discipline, who speak a specific technical language, who identify with the topic, and who have a passion for the subject. When you get a group of geologists in a bar, they tend to talk geology all night. This is the sort of interest, energy and identification with the topic, which will really hold a community together.

The other side of the coin is that there is no point in setting up communities that cover temporary work, part-time work, or tasks that people are not particularly interested in. One engineering company attempted to set up a community of people who prepared a particular form of baseline plan. However, this was not their full-time job, it was not their core competency, it was not something they were particularly interested in, much of the work was done by contractors, and as soon as the job was finished they would move on to something different and more attractive. There was no interest from the practitioners in forming a community about baseline planning, because they just did not identify with the topic.

The company will therefore be most successful in building communities where there is already a sense of identity, and one of the key tasks of the community coordinator will be to build and foster a sense of identity.

Community coordinator

The community of practice needs a defined coordinator. This is the person who is accountable for the smooth operation of the community of practice. Some of the responsibilities of the coordinator are listed below:

- managing the community discussions (online, and face to face);
- making sure agreed community behaviours are followed;
- setting up the community meetings;
- working with the core group;
- liaising with subject matter experts;
- watching for problems where knowledge sharing is not happening;
- maintaining the membership list;
- representing the community to management;

- managing the lifecycle of the community;
- keeping energy levels high among participants, to ensure active participation.

The community coordinator does not necessarily manage the knowledge of the community. As discussed above, the organisational knowledge is often managed by subject matter experts (Chapter 4), and it helps if the community coordinator is not themselves a recognised guru or expert. Their job is to make sure the knowledge of the community is managed, not necessarily to manage it themselves.

The most important attributes for the community coordinator are passion and energy. The coordinator of the community acts as the dynamo for the community, keeping energy levels high and positive. The community coordinator needs to be an insider; they need to be a member of the organisation, they need to be well-known and well-respected, and they need to be a practitioner in the topic. They have to understand the jargon and the language, and they have to know the key players. The community leaders can be appointed (as in Buckman Laboratories); they can be nominated by the community (as in Shell); or they can emerge as the natural leader based on their passion and energy (as in some BP communities). They can be called coordinators, or facilitators, or leaders, or minders; whatever terminology is acceptable to the community.

In a small community, the coordinator role may be a part-time role. In a larger community, say of greater than 500 members, the coordinator role should be full-time. This is especially true if the community knowledge is of strategic value. There may be additional roles in a larger community, some of which are described below:

- content coordinator, to look after the community website;
- technical support for community knowledge sharing tools;
- occasional logistics and secretarial support for arranging community meetings;
- a core community membership, who are active in asking and answering questions and in sharing knowledge;
- peripheral members, who are part of the community but rarely offer their knowledge;
- lurkers, who are members of the community that never take part in discussion;
- people who span the boundaries with other communities.

The community coordinator needs to coordinate the activity of all of these people, and also of the subject matter experts.

Subject matter experts

The subject matter experts (also known as knowledge area owners) own and manage the knowledge of specific topics on behalf of the community. For example, the legal community in an organisation may nominate different experts to manage the knowledge of contract law, Internet law, employment law and so on. They are recognised practitioners in that topic area, who have credibility, experience and authority. They can speak on behalf of the community, and make the decisions about which knowledge is valid and which is not. The role of the subject matter experts is described above.

A launch meeting

The best way to start up a community of practice is to hold a launch meeting. Here you bring the potential core community members together, and work with them to design with the way the community will operate. Obviously before you invest in a launch meeting, you will have some idea that the community of practice will add value through sharing knowledge. You will realise that there is knowledge to be shared, that the organisation is currently operating inefficiently due to poor access to knowledge, and that the community of practice will be a key component of the knowledge sharing system you put together. You may have to make a business case to somebody in management, to release funds for a launch meeting. You will already have identified the nature of the knowledge that is needed, and therefore the nature of the community, and you will already have identified the key knowledge-holders and knowledge-users in that community. You will also have identified some of the optional processes and technologies that the community might use to share knowledge. Once you have done all this, it is time to hold a launch meeting. The launch meeting will cover the following:

- *Business context for the community.* Articulate the business reason. What are the efficiency gains from sharing knowledge in the community? How much time or money could the community save by sharing what they know? What are the potential new opportunities? How does the community fit with company strategy?

■ *Introduction to knowledge management.* Because the rest of the workshop will be about knowledge exchange, and building systems for knowledge exchange, it is important to talk around some of the concepts, and to develop a common language. Try if possible to tell some relevant success stories with which the attendees can identify, and give them a vision of what it could be like in a world with instant access to operational knowledge. Hearing from the successes of others, will help them visualise what a community can do for them. This session is about developing a shared vision of what is possible. So, you need to set this session up as a visioning session – not something to listen to passively, but an opportunity to explore possibilities.

■ *If you have time, do some first-pass knowledge exchange.* The purpose of this part of the meeting is to demonstrate to the participants that 'other people do have knowledge which can be useful to you'. There are a number of ways you can organise this section of the meeting, but the purpose is:

  – to show people the range of knowledge, expertise and good practice that is available in the community;

  – to build some trust among the community, by showing that people know what they are talking about; and

  – to show that not everyone knows everything, and that there is benefit in sharing with each other.

■ *Develop a draft terms of reference.* You will have developed some close relationships in the kick-off meeting, and will have formed the basis of trust, respect and knowledge-awareness that will form the foundation for your community of practice. The attendees, now a nascent community, need to agree the processes for keeping the community alive once the meeting is over. They will need to appoint a coordinator and other roles, choose a communication mechanism, determine a meetings schedule, and begin a discussion on terms of reference (see below). They will need to start up a membership list, and develop a plan for enrolling other members.

Critical mass

The community needs to develop a critical mass. Communities of practice need a certain amount of interaction going on, to remain in the consciousness of the community members. They can suffer from 'out of sight, out of mind', and the community which is too small or too preoccupied to be sufficiently active will begin to lose its sense of identity, and people will forget it is there. Active online communities probably need at least one message a day on their message board or in their Q&A forum.

The community coordinator therefore needs to build membership and grow the community as fast as possible after launch, to keep the momentum going, and to get to critical mass as soon as possible. This will require a combination of marketing, advertising, awareness-raising, and direct invitation to people who might be interested. This is likely to take a considerable portion of the community coordinator's time in the first few months after launch. Each potential new member needs to be welcomed into the community, introduced to the terms of reference, and encouraged to take part in knowledge-sharing.

The size of the critical mass varies on the intensity of the learning, the passion of the individuals, and how diverse they are culturally and geographically. For a co-located community of passionate experts working in a new field, the critical mass may be a dozen people. For a global community working in an established field, exchanging knowledge through e-mail and online, the critical mass may be several hundred people.

Discussion forums

The primary way for community members to access community knowledge is through asking questions. Any community member, facing a problem in their project where they lack complete knowledge, should have a means of asking the community for help, and of receiving answers.

In a co-located community, this can be done in regular face-to-face meetings. For example the communities of practice ('tech clubs') in the Chrysler Auburn Hill plant, meet weekly or fortnightly to solve problems and exchange good practices. A worker working on brake systems for Jeeps may have a problem, which he can raise at the 'braking systems' tech club, and receive answers from people working on braking systems in vans, small cars, etc.

Communities of practice in dispersed or multi-national businesses cannot meet regularly on a face-to-face basis. They need some virtual means of raising questions and receiving answers. There are very many web-based or e-mail-based forums that allow just this facility, and these are proven and popular tools for sharing knowledge within communities.

Shell, for example, run three large communities of practice in their upstream business – one for drillers and well engineers, one for geologists, geophysicists and other subsurface staff, and one for facilities engineers. Anyone with a need for knowledge can send a message to the online community notice board, and every day a daily e-mail prompt is sent to the membership, alerting them of any new questions that have been asked. Any community member who can answer one of the questions will generally write back with useful advice, if they have the time. The combination of a web-based repository for the questions and answers, with an e-mail alert system, is a powerful combination, used by many companies. This is much better than reliance on the web alone, and on community members logging on to look for new questions. (This approach doesn't seem to have sustainable longevity, and people seem to quickly get out of the habit.) Community questions and answers need to be accessed using the daily communication tools of the community members, whether these are the web, e-mail, meetings, or telephone. An e-mail based question and answer form is given in Figure 4.9.

A way to find each other

Communities must be visible. Project staff must be able to find relevant communities, they must be able to join them easily, and they must be able to see who else is a community member. There should ideally be, in the organisation, some index or Yellow Pages for the communities. In BP, this function is provided by BP Connect, the Yellow Pages system, where each community has a page where it sets out its aims and objectives, lists the community members, and allows you to join or leave the community with one mouse-click.

A place to store common property

If the community of practice takes ownership of the cross-project knowledge (as discussed above), then it needs somewhere to store and share the best practices, knowledge assets and company standards. This is likely to be a community website.

So, for example, the knowledge management community in one retail organisation run their own website to develop and share knowledge about managing knowledge. The Engineers within BP Major Projects have a website called 'Engineering Technical Practices', where they store validated standards best practices, and lessons learned.

Figure 4.9 Screenshot from a community discussion forum

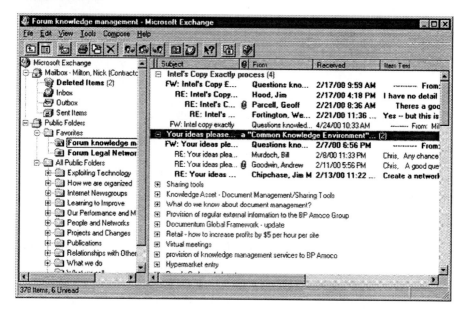

In a large, technology-enabled and technology-focused community, the community knowledge base can become very sophisticated. The InTouchSupport.com system in Schlumberger, for example, cost $160 million to develop as a knowledge base to store and share knowledge on technical solutions. However, because technology support is Schlumberger's main business, the company felt that this resource was worthwhile. By cutting 95 per cent from the time it takes to answer a technical question, they feel it adds an annual value of $200 million. This gives Schlumberger staff the ability to solve technical problems very rapidly, in a business where time is money.

Terms of reference

A 'Terms of reference' sets the ground rules for the community of practice, and is the defining document. It describes what the community is about, and how it works. Terms of reference are for the benefit of potential members, so they know what they are joining, and for existing members, to remind them of why they are a community.

The terms of reference need to define at least the following four components.

- *The aims of the community.* This should define what the community is for, and what is its high-level purpose. It should also define the scope of the knowledge that the community will exchange. For example, the aims of an electrical engineering community might be 'to add value to project work across the organisation, by giving project engineers immediate access to the knowledge of their peers, in the area of electrical engineering'.

- *The objectives of the community.* This should define what the community is attempting to achieve in the short to medium term.

- *The process by which the community will operate and share knowledge.* This should include a description of the technologies that will be used, the question and answer forum, the index of members, the defined roles, the websites for community knowledge, and so on.

- *The principles by which the community will operate,* such as openness, generosity with knowledge, lack of criticism, and so on. For example, the Well Engineering community in Shell have a list of community behaviours which include items like 'support and never criticise', 'equal rights and status for contractors and Shell staff' and 'celebrate every success'.

Defining the terms of reference can be very useful exercise at the community launch event (see earlier).

A social network

The members of a community are happy to share knowledge with each other because they feel a sense of identity with each other, and they are even happier to share knowledge with community members that they know personally and feel a social connection with. Much work has been done in the field of knowledge management on the concept of social network analysis. This involves mapping out the social links and the interactions within a community, in order to assess the level of connectivity of the individuals. Certainly the community coordinator should be using any means possible to improve social connectivity, such as face-to-face meetings (see below). Social connectivity forms the groundwork for developing trust within the community, and trust is an essential ingredient if knowledge is to be shared and re-used.

However, assured and systematic knowledge management needs to transcend the social networks, and needs to develop processes and approaches for accessing the knowledge of people you don't know and have never met. Approaches such as the question and answer forum, described above, allow knowledge sharing to take place within an entire community, regardless of how socially connected the individuals may be.

Face-to-face meetings

The best way to develop sociability and trust, is for the members of the community to meet on a fairly regular basis. This ideally should be at least annually, and should involve the core active members of the community. The meeting can be based around knowledge-sharing, and can help set the coming year's objectives for the community.

Wherever possible, the meeting should avoid being the standard agenda of PowerPoint presentations. It's far better to mix some knowledge sharing (such as getting the community to collectively brainstorm some problem areas for specific projects, or to collectively build a best practice) with some more socially-based activity (making sure people sit with people they have never met before, moving people round to different tables, icebreakers and introduction games), and with some activities designed to strengthen the functioning of the community after the workshop is finished (revisiting the terms of reference, redesigning the website, etc.)

A level of autonomy

In allowing communities of practice to exist and operate, the organisation is accepting that much of the knowledge lies with the practitioners, and can effectively be shared between the practitioners. The organisation must therefore give the practitioners enough autonomy to act on the knowledge they receive. They should be empowered to use best practice that has been validated by the community, without necessarily getting their line manager to re-validate it every time. This does not mean that all decision making is delegated to community members, but it means that line management can delegate a certain level of technical assurance to the communities. Disempowered communities rapidly become cynical and disaffected, which can become a bigger problem for management than having no communities at all.

Yellow Pages systems

Earlier in this chapter we introduced the idea of a Yellow Pages system for indexing communities of practice. This is only one part of the functionality of a Yellow Pages system that might be introduced to facilitate cross-project exchange of knowledge.

A Yellow Pages system might be defined as an index of what people do and what people know. The analogy is, of course, with the *Yellow Pages* commercial telephone directory, where people and business are indexed according to the services they provided, rather (in the normal 'white pages' telephone directory) than according to their name. A Yellow Pages system in an organisation may provide the same sort of functionality. Where the corporate telephone directory provides the 'white pages', the Yellow Pages will provide an index of what people know and what they do. So, for example, in the Yellow Pages, you should be able to search for all the lawyers in the company, or all the lawyers specialising in Internet law, or all the lawyers specialising in Internet law who are based in Houston, Texas.

The Yellow Pages system provides project team members with a way of finding people with expertise, who may be able to solve specific problems. For example, a project engineer may be working with a shipyard in the early stages of designing a marine surveying vessel, and may have a specific question about a technical aspect of design. One way of looking for knowledge to help answer this question would be to go to the company Yellow Pages system, and search for people with expertise in designing marine survey vessels. He could then e-mail the people he found with a query, or telephone some of them, or invite them to a peer assist.

In a large global organisation, with many projects happening simultaneously around the world, a Yellow Pages system can be very powerful. Nobody in the company can know everybody else; nobody in the company can rely on their personal social network to connect them with all the internal expertise that exists. The Yellow Pages acts as an index of the tacit knowledge of the organisation. For example, BP has in the order of 100,000 staff worldwide, who collectively hold over a million working-years of experience. The company Yellow Pages system, BP Connect, indexes much of this knowledge and experience. Although registration on Connect is entirely voluntary, over 33,500 people had registered as of August 2004, many of them sharing their personal details and a photograph as well as details of their expertise. A search of the system allows you to find, for example, the nine people with experience of paraxylene crystallisation process technology, the 18 people who know about qualitative holistic risk assessment in project management, and the single person working on military fuels. For project team members searching for obscure specialist knowledge, this can be an incredibly valuable tool.

When an organisation considers introducing Yellow Pages, there is often a debate as to whether population of the details should be voluntary (as in the BP case) or mandatory, and whether the details should be populated by the users, or by some other means (such as HR, or auto-population through mining e-mail traffic). Which approach you choose may depend to a large extent on your corporate culture, but the voluntary approach is probably best. It is hard to mandate knowledge management – knowledge needs to be offered voluntarily, and re-used willingly. It is better to help people to want to do it, rather than to force them.

Notes

1. By 'lesson learned' we mean a piece of advice that suggests 'under these circumstances and in this context, there is a practice which we recommend that you adopt, based on our experience in this particular project'.
2. By 'best practice', we mean a piece of advice that suggests 'under these circumstances and in this context, there is a practice which we recommend that you adopt, as it has frequently proven in the past to be the best course of action'.
3. By 'company standard' we mean an approach that should be adopted throughout the company, except where there is a very good justification for doing something different.
4. Some companies don't like to use the term 'best practice'. they feel that a practice need not necessarily ever be the best in all circumstances, or they may feel that the concept of 'best' might alienate people ('What makes them think that their practice is best?'). One engineering company found that the term 'best practice' was used as a defence against learning new approaches ('We can't use your idea, we will stick with established best practice'). These reasons are not necessarily failures of the terminology – they may instead be failures of the validation and update process. However, there are alternative names. You can call them 'good practices', 'better practices', or 'proven practices' if you prefer.

5

Assurance and embedding

The topic of *assurance* is one that needs to be addressed when implementing any sort of management system. By 'assurance' we mean, how can an organisation be sure that the system is being used, and is being used to best effect?

If we assume that knowledge management delivers value to project work, how can the organisation be sure that projects will manage their knowledge properly in order to deliver that value? Knowledge management is too important to leave to the ad hoc goodwill of project teams. It needs a systematic approach, embedded into business and project processes, with an assurance system by which the organisation can know that it is being applied to full effect.

There are up to five elements that can be combined into an assurance system for knowledge management within projects:

- a strategic knowledge management framework for the organisation;
- knowledge management standards for the projects;
- knowledge management plans for individual projects;
- knowledge management assessments or audits for individual projects;
- a company-wide measurement and reporting system for knowledge management.

Knowledge management strategic elements

Any organisation that wishes to apply management knowledge with a full level of organisational assurance needs to define a strategic framework for knowledge management within and between the projects. A strategic framework is a system for ensuring that knowledge is managed consistently, systematically and strategically, in a standardised and sustainable manner. A suitable framework is shown in Figure 5.1 and consists of the following strategic elements:

- Five strategic elements set by senior management, which define the expectations set for the projects and cross-project groups.

  - A corporate vision for knowledge management, which sets the context for the rest of the framework. This vision describes what knowledge management will lead towards, and defines the purpose for knowledge management within the organisation.

  - A corporate strategy for knowledge management, which sets out a specific directional approach for knowledge management.

  - Corporate standards for knowledge management, within the projects and within the cross-project area (the networks and communities, the disciplines and functions, and the specialist areas). These standards will cover elements such as knowledge management plans, standards for developing and maintaining knowledge assets, standards for community management, and so on (see the next section).

Figure 5.1 A framework of strategic elements for knowledge management in a project-focused organisation

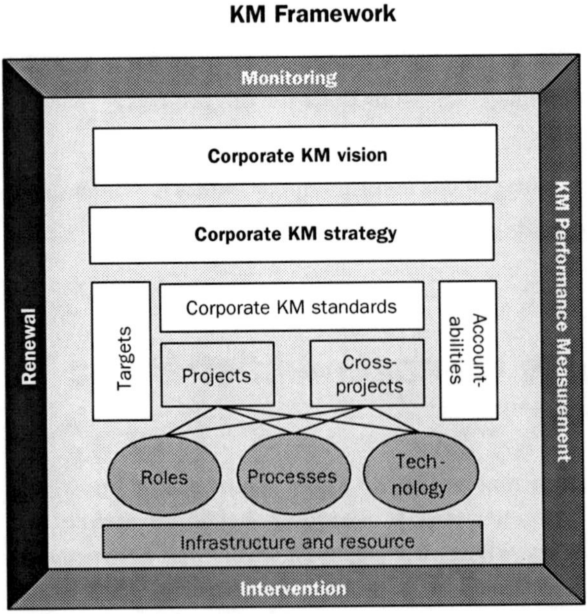

KM Framework

- A chain of clear delegated accountabilities for implementing the standards, within the projects and within the cross-project area.
- A set of performance targets to accompany these accountabilities.

■ Strategic elements that define the enabling structures which need to be in place to allow the capture, storage and exchange of knowledge.

- A defined set of roles, processes, and technology tools for managing knowledge. A range of suitable roles, processes and technologies are described in Chapters 3 and 4.
- An infrastructure to support the roles, processes and technologies. This will include an IT infrastructure, an IM infrastructure, a training infrastructure, and a set of reference resources.

■ A system for ensuring the continued effective operation of knowledge management. This system is likely to be operated by a knowledge management support team – as will be described in further detail later in this chapter, and will include:

- monitoring knowledge management deployment and application;
- measuring the performance of knowledge management within the organisation;
- making any interventions required to deliver the framework; and
- renewing any of the framework elements as the business context changes.

Knowledge management standards

As one of the strategic elements, the organisation needs to define the expected standard approach to be applied to knowledge management within the projects, and applied to management of knowledge between the projects.

Project-level knowledge management standards

These define the minimum conditions of satisfaction for management of knowledge within the projects. If the project doesn't follow this standard approach, the project manager is not doing their job.

An example set of standards might be as follows.

- Knowledge inputs to the project have been identified, the sources of this knowledge have been identified, and owned actions are in place to acquire the knowledge.

- Major areas of knowledge creation from the project have been identified, and owned actions are in place to capture and document this knowledge on behalf of the wider organisation beyond the immediate project.

- A project knowledge management plan (see below) is established for the project, covering the two items above.

- An owner for this plan has been appointed, and their performance contract amended to reflect the new accountability.

- Project staff have been trained in the knowledge management system, and are signed up to any relevant networks.

- In-project and cross-project knowledge stores and lessons databases have been identified and put in place, with clear processes to keep the content current and validated.

- All key learning activities (such as retrospects and peer assists) are in the project plan, and scheduled for each of the project phases.

Cross-project knowledge management standards

The organisation also needs to define a set of standard expectations for the cross-project management of knowledge (whether this is done within the networks, the disciplines or functions, or within a central group, as discussed in Chapter 4).

An example set of standards might be as follows.

- Strategic knowledge areas for the organisation have been identified, and cross-project ownership of these areas has been assigned.

- Subject matter experts are in place for all key areas of knowledge.

- Communities of practice are in place for all key knowledge practice areas.

- Best practices and standards are in place for all key areas of knowledge.

- A suitable update schedule is in place for these best practices and standards, including a notification process for any updates.

- A cross-project lessons learned database is in place and owned.

- A housekeeping process is in place for this lessons learned database, to ensure old lessons are cleared out.

- All subject matter experts and community coordinators have been trained in knowledge management, and are part of the knowledge management community of practice.

Knowledge management plans

The concept of a project-level knowledge management plan is one of the most exciting new ideas to come out of knowledge management in the past five years. It is a device that allows knowledge management to be fully embedded into project controls, at the same level of rigour as risk management, or document management. It allows the assignment of accountabilities to individual project team members, and allows these accountabilities to be monitored and reviewed. Knowledge management plans allow knowledge management to evolve to become a true management discipline, a component part of an integrated project management approach rather than an add-on or an aspiration.

A knowledge management plan is a document for a specific project, which details:

- what knowledge is *needed* by the project;

- what knowledge will be *created* by the project;

- what *system* of processes, technologies and roles will be used to manage knowledge within the project,;

- what *actions* need to be taken to implement the system; and

- which *people* are accountable for individual actions.

Project-level knowledge management plans have been applied in relatively few places, and the details of their application are still evolving, but it seems likely that a robust knowledge management plan will contain three elements, shown in Figure 5.2. The three elements of a knowledge management plan are as follows:

1. *A knowledge management system*, which defines the way in which knowledge will be managed in the project. It defines the roles that will be needed, the technologies (such as lessons databases) that will be

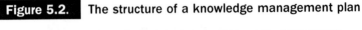

Figure 5.2. The structure of a knowledge management plan

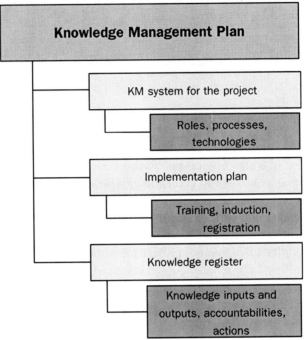

used, and the processes that will be applied (and also, when they will be applied). The knowledge management system for the project will need to conform to corporate knowledge management standards, and it is quite likely that all projects within a single business will conform to a common system.

2. *An implementation plan for the project,* to make sure the system is ready to use. This will require training staff in the tools and technologies, inducting new staff, registering staff with the relevant communities of practice, installing necessary technology onto people's desktops, and so on.

3. *A knowledge register,* which defines the key areas of knowledge needed by the project ('knowledge inputs'), the key areas of knowledge which the project will be learning about and which they need to share with the rest of the organisation ('knowledge outputs'), and the actions which need to be assigned to make sure these inputs and outputs actually happen.

A knowledge management plan therefore takes the broad topic of knowledge management, and turns it into a specific definition, tailored for the project, of who should be doing what, by when, using which tools, in order to manage knowledge for the benefit of the project, and for the benefit of the company. As an analogy, a project knowledge management plan contains the same degree of detail, process and rigour as a project risk management plan. Knowledge and risk are two of the main intangibles that need to be managed through the project. A discussion of the interface between knowledge management and risk management can be found in Chapter 6.

Creating the knowledge management plan

One of the best approaches to creating a knowledge management plan, is to do it at a workshop for the project team. At the workshop, the team can be introduced to the tools and processes that the project might adopt, they can work through the key knowledge areas, and they can assign and accept actions. At the end of the workshop, the input material for the knowledge management plan will all be ready, and the plan can be constructed by the project knowledge manager.

A typical agenda for a knowledge management planning workshop is shown in Panel 5.1.

If it is not possible to bring the team together for a knowledge management planning workshop, then the knowledge manager will have to do much of the work themselves, in one-on-one discussion with the other team members. However, at the very least, the team need to be brought together for an hour or two, to discuss 'what is knowledge management?' and to brainstorm the knowledge inputs and outputs of the project.

Defining the knowledge needs and inputs

The easiest way to define the knowledge needs and inputs for a project, is through a group discussion with the project team members. You can start this process by making the point that knowledge is a required asset for successful performance. To do any project you will need resources, one resource being knowledge. You need people resources, financial resources, and knowledge resources. It is therefore useful to think about the knowledge inputs to a project. The knowledge inputs are those areas

---

Panel 5.1: Knowledge management planning workshop agenda

Day 1

08:30	Introduction, objectives	
08:45	knowledge management principles and framework	Presentation and discussion Group work
09:30	Project current status	
10:15	Coffee	
10:30	Knowledge management simulation exercise	Group work
12:30	Lunch	
13:00	Knowledge communication and communities	Presentation and discussion
13:30	Project knowledge inputs and outputs	Group work
14:15	Knowledge capture	Presentation and discussion
14:45	Coffee	
15:00	Capture processes	Group work
15:45	Project knowledge storage	Presentation and discussion
16:15	Technology hands-on	Group work
17:00	Finish	

Day 2

08:30	Implementation issues	Presentation and discussion
09:00	The knowledge management system	Group work
10:00	Implementation actions	Group work
10:30	Coffee	
10:45	Knowledge management register	Group work
12:00	Lunch	

---

of knowledge that the project team needs to know about, in order to deliver their objectives. You need to find out from the project team, what do they need to know? What know-how do they need to acquire in order to complete the project? What knowledge resources are critical to success?

If you are doing this in a workshop, then write at the top of a flipchart 'We need to know how to ...'. Then ask the project team members to supply 10–20 of the most important key areas that are vital to the project. Encourage them to stay away from very small, detailed activities and look for the more high-level strategic ones. For example, they may respond with 'We need to know how to deliver safe road transport' or 'We need to know how to negotiate effectively with the client'. If the team members are finding it hard to get started, given them an example or two like the above.

There may be a strong link with the risk management exercise. Many of the areas of knowledge are needed in order to address the risks that will have been identified. It therefore makes sense to do the knowledge management planning after the project risk planning.

If the team members are tempted to get into a debate about the knowledge not being available, tell them not to think about this for now – all you need at this stage is identification of the key knowledge inputs.

Ranking the knowledge needs and inputs

Not all the knowledge needs and inputs for the project are of equal importance, and not all of the knowledge can be acquired in the same way. So, the brainstorming exercise described above can be usefully followed by a ranking exercise. A good way to rank the knowledge needs is by importance, and by availability. You can give the project team members a set of ranking criteria, for example as in Table 5.1, to allow them to assign numerical ranks to the different knowledge needs.

Once the team members have given these two scores to the knowledge, it allows you to cross plot the individual knowledge inputs on a Boston Square Matrix, as shown in Figure 5.3. This allows you to rank your knowledge inputs into four main categories.

The four main categories are as follows.

1. Knowledge areas which are very important to the project, but where the knowledge does not exist, or is not easily available, fall within the CREATE box of the matrix. The project must create this knowledge for itself. For example, a project may require some innovative technology that will need to be developed or invented. The project may use an approach such as business-driven action learning (see Chapter 3) as a way of creating this knowledge. Once created, the

Table 5.1   Knowledge input ranking criteria

How important is this knowledge to the project?	To what extent does this knowledge exist?
5 – Absolutely vital: if we don't acquire this knowledge we will fail	5 – The knowledge is out there, we just need to go find it
4 – Extremely important: if we don't acquire this knowledge we be at very serious disadvantage	4 – Most of the knowledge is there if we look for it
3 – Very important: this is a key component of making the project work	3 – Some of the knowledge exists, some of it doesn't
2 – Important: this knowledge will help make the project work	2 – Only the first few bits of knowledge are in place
1 – Useful: this knowledge could be helpful to us	1 – This is unknown territory for everyone

knowledge needs to be captured for future use by this and subsequent projects. Someone on the project will need to take accountability for running this knowledge creation activity, and the subsequent knowledge capture.

2. Knowledge areas which are very important to the project, but where the knowledge is available, fall within the COLLECT box of the matrix. Here the project can invest in some learning from others, in order to bring the knowledge into the project. Approaches such as peer assists (Chapter 3) and the involvement of communities of practice (Chapter 4) can be employed as a means of collecting the required knowledge. With any luck, some knowledge assets (Chapter 4) may already exist, and there may be company standards (Chapter 4) or lessons learned databases (Chapter 4) that can provide guidance.

3. Knowledge areas which are not very important to the project, and where the knowledge is easily available, are not going to be a high priority to the project team. If the knowledge is useful, however, they

Figure 5.3	Boston Square Matrix: categorisation of key knowledge areas

High level of importance	**CREATE** The crucial knowledge does not exist. You need to go out and create it. Make sure you have learning processes in place	**COLLECT** The crucial knowledge does exist. You need to go out and collect it. Find out where it is, and choose suitable processes to find and in place store it
Low level of importance	**WATCH** Keep a watching brief on these areas	**OUTSOURCE** This knowledge exists – why not get someone else to collect it for you, or buy in the knowledge through contractors or consultants

Low level of availability   High level of availability

may rely on others to collect the knowledge for them. They could hire consultants with the required knowledge, or they could sponsor small knowledge collection exercises. This box has therefore been labelled *OUTSOURCE*.

4. Knowledge areas which are not very important to the project, but where the knowledge doesn't exist anyway, fall into the box marked *WATCH*. Here the project team may want to keep a watching brief, in case this knowledge is created (perhaps by their competitors) and turns out to be more important than they thought.

As an example, a project team working on new technology recently went through this exercise. Many of their knowledge areas (variant and subsets of 'how will this technology work in practice') fell into the CREATE box. However, there were a significant number of knowledge areas (e.g. 'what are our competitors doing in this area?') that fell into the COLLECT box, and there were also some areas (e.g. 'how will the public react to this technology') which fell into the WATCHING BRIEF box. This exercise allowed them to assign some actions to team members to set in place some knowledge collection exercises, and allowed them to sense check their pilot projects against the knowledge creation needs.

Defining the knowledge outputs

Projects also generate knowledge. Not only will the project create monetary value, it can also create knowledge value, so long as that knowledge is captured. This is particularly true when the project is covering a new area, where a considerable amount of new knowledge could be created for the organisation. You therefore need to discuss with the project team not only what knowledge the project needs, but what knowledge the project will create. This discussion can be combined with the discussion above about knowledge inputs, or it can be held immediately afterwards. In a workshop format, you can write at the top of a flipchart 'We are (will be) learning how to ...'. Then ask the delegates to supply five of the most important key knowledge areas where they will be gaining knowledge in current or future activity. For example, they may respond with 'We will be working for the first time with the Algerian government', or 'we will be investigating the use of tension-leg platforms'.

You may want to rank these knowledge areas in order of importance for the rest of the organisation, although the project team may not be the best placed people to comment on this.

Building the knowledge register

Once the knowledge areas have been identified, you need to start thinking about how that knowledge will be managed, and building up a knowledge register for the project. For each of the knowledge areas (whether input or output) you need to decide who is going to look after that area of knowledge, and what they are going to do with it. You can do this within the knowledge management planning workshop, or through one-on-one discussions. However you choose to do it, there is a series of steps to take, and questions to be answered.

1. *What is the crucial knowledge?* This is a restatement of the knowledge area which needs to be managed.
2. *At which project stage is this knowledge needed?* This will help in prioritising knowledge input, and will allow stage-by-stage review of the register.

3. *Where will this knowledge come from?* If it is available, it will come from some external source, such as a previous project, an in-house expert, or a community or practice. If it is unavailable, then the project team will need to create it as part of the project.

4. *Which knowledge process would you use to access this knowledge?* Once you have identified the source of the knowledge, then you need to choose the best means to access that knowledge. Example answers to this question might be 'we need to run a peer assist with the people from the Middle Eastern business unit', or 'we need to sign up to the procurement community', or 'we need to find the corporate best practices for contract strategy'.

5. *Who is accountable for accessing this knowledge?* Someone needs to take action, to make sure the knowledge is accessed. This won't be the job of the knowledge manager – it will be the job of the most obvious person. For example, if 'contract strategy' is a key area of knowledge, then the person who needs to get hold of that knowledge would be the contracts specialist on the project.

6. *Action.* The action for accessing the knowledge needs to be defined, and dated.

7. *Which knowledge process would you use to capture this knowledge?* When the knowledge has been accessed by the team, and applied within the project, then their own experiences with this knowledge need to be captured and fed back to the organisation. How will this be done? Will it be done through a retrospect, or by writing a file-note, or by uploading a lesson to the corporate lessons database?

8. *Who is accountable for capturing this knowledge?* Again, this won't be the job of the knowledge manager, although the knowledge manager may facilitate the process. Again, using the example of contracting strategy, it will be the contracts specialist who captures any new knowledge on contracts, and feeds that back to the contracts community, or to the relevant subject matter expert.

9. *Action.* The action for capturing the knowledge needs to be defined, and dated.

10. *Output.* When the action has been completed, the location of the output document, or relevant lesson, can be recorded in the knowledge register.

Tracking the actions

Building the knowledge register results in a list of actions. This is one of the great benefits of the knowledge management planning exercise; it results in immediate identified actions associated with key areas of knowledge, and therefore takes what might otherwise seem to be an esoteric topic (knowledge management) and makes it into something very practical. The status of the actions needs to be monitored by the project knowledge manager. If the project already has an action log, then the knowledge management actions can be combined with this.

Defining the knowledge management system for the project

The four steps described above take as a starting point the identified knowledge inputs and outputs for the project, and track these through into actions for managing this knowledge. These actions each address one single area of knowledge. There also needs to be a section in the knowledge management plan where all these actions are brought together into an integrated knowledge management system for the project. This section needs to answer the following questions:

- What regular knowledge management processes will be adopted by the team, and how will they be integrated into the project timeline? For example, at what stage, and with what frequency, will the team adopt after action reviews? When does the team plan to hold regular retrospects?

- What technologies will the team use to store their lessons, and track their knowledge management actions?

- Who, on the team, will be taking a knowledge management role for the project?

- Which are the communities of practice into which the project team needs to link?

- What are the lessons learned databases or best practice compilations that the project team needs to use for reference?

This exercise defines the flow of knowledge into and out of the project, without reference to the specific knowledge content for knowledge areas. It defines the routine knowledge management practices of the team, rather than the management of specific critical knowledge areas. An

Figure 5.4 Example knowledge management system for a project

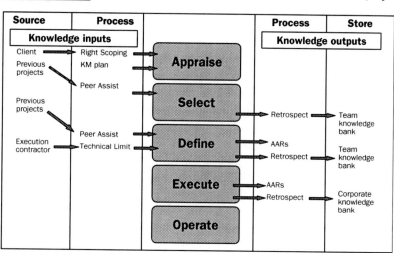

example system is shown as Figure 5.4 – in this case as a flow diagram showing the flow of knowledge into and out from the project.

Defining the implementation plan

The team may not yet be ready to start managing knowledge using the system defined above. There may be some set-up or training needed. It is a good idea, as part of the knowledge management planning, to run some sort of audit or check of the state of the art of knowledge management within the team, and list the actions needed to bring the team up to speed. Some of the following actions may be needed:

- Educate the team in the processes and technologies that will be used to manage knowledge during the project.
- Make sure the team members have got access to all the lessons learned databases and other knowledge resources that will be used during the project.
- Make sure the team members have joined the relevant communities of practice.
- Make sure that each team member has updated their profile in the corporate Yellow Pages.

These actions can also be added to the team action log.

The knowledge management plan as a living document

Creating the knowledge management plan is itself a useful exercise, but if the plan is to deliver real value then it needs to be a living document. The plan needs to be owned by somebody, namely the person in the team who has been given responsibility for knowledge management. This person is most likely to be the defined knowledge manager for the team (Chapter 3). The knowledge manager will use the knowledge management plan throughout the project in the following ways:

- The knowledge management plan should be used for tracking any actions that come out of the team learning processes. The knowledge register is used as an assurance document to make sure that actions are carried out, and therefore that lessons are being learned and implemented. For example, the knowledge management plan may identify that knowledge of contracting strategy is crucial to the project, and that knowledge is best acquired through a peer assist with three previous projects, to learn from their contracting strategy. Someone will have been given the accountability for organising this in the knowledge register, and the knowledge manager can track that this action is taking place. However, there will also be actions arising from the peer assist itself. The visiting teams may suggest that the project should make changes to its contracting strategy, perhaps adding an incentive programme for the main contractor. The action of making these changes should also be added to the project action log, and the knowledge manager can track that this action is closed out. The plan therefore is a document that ensures that learning is acquired and acted upon.

- The knowledge management plan is used as the definition document for knowledge management activities within the programme. It should point the reader to any relevant reference material, and it should define which activities will be taking place during the life of the project. Any changes in the level of knowledge management activities need to be reflected by changes in the plan.

- The knowledge management plan can be used by the project gatekeeper to track the application of knowledge management within the project, at the stage gate reviews. This provides a mechanism for assuring the quality of the knowledge management process. For example, at a stage-gate review between the options selection stage and the detailed design stage, the gatekeeper might check that:

- all key knowledge from the options selection stage has been captured, that all 'capture actions' from this stage have been closed out, and that all output documentation has been placed in the appropriate place, and
- all key knowledge for the detailed design stage has been accessed, and that all 'access actions' for this stage have been closed out.

■ New critical knowledge areas may arise during the life of the project. These could be identified in after action reviews or retrospects, in meetings with senior managers, or could come out of the parallel risk management process. The knowledge manager needs to ensure that these new areas are owned and entered into the knowledge register, and that there are actions in place to manage these new knowledge areas.

Knowledge management monitoring and assurance

The framework of strategic elements shown in Figure 5.1 is surrounded by a layer labelled 'monitoring, knowledge management performance management, interventions and renewal'. This layer represents the structure that needs to be in place to provide a constant overview of the effectiveness of knowledge management within and between the projects, to make sure that the organisation has the resources and training it needs, and to instigate any interventions if the standard of knowledge management may start to decline.

Monitoring and measuring can take place at several levels:

■ measuring the level of deployment of knowledge management standards and approaches across the organisation;

■ measuring the effectiveness of the knowledge management framework in allowing the flow of knowledge between projects;

■ measuring the level of knowledge-sharing activity within the knowledge management system.

Assessment of the level of deployment

Especially during the roll-out of the knowledge management, it is necessary to measure the level of deployment across the different business units. For example, a mining company used a nine-stage scale to measure the degree of knowledge management application in the business units, which can be summarised as follows:

1. No contact with knowledge management.

2. Initial contact and training, but no activity.

3. Initial training of core group, knowledge manager identified, first trial of knowledge management activity.

4. Training spreading to the rest of the business unit, knowledge manager in place, knowledge management activity trials continue.

5. Knowledge manager fully trained, business unit has adopted a knowledge management system, first knowledge assets being created.

6. Business unit leadership in full support of knowledge management system, demonstrable continuous improvement through knowledge management, business-scale best practices identified.

7. Knowledge management fully embedded in all business unit projects, business unit leadership taking the lead to promote knowledge management in other business units. Significant transfer of knowledge to other business units.

8. Knowledge management fully built into the performance management and reward system, clear evidence of knowledge-based continuous improvement of repeat projects.

9 Knowledge management fully internalised in the business unit culture, leadership tasking a proactive role in delivering value through cross-business unit knowledge management.

By tracking the scores for each of the business units, they were able to monitor the take-up of knowledge management across the different business, and to track the spread of the discipline.

BP Gulf of Mexico uses a simpler traffic-light system to measure the deployment of knowledge management tools and behaviours, with red, yellow and green representing no deployment, partial deployment and full deployment.

Deployment can also be measured at individual and team level. Prior to knowledge management planning workshops in a business with an established knowledge management system, we have recently been surveying project team members to gauge their familiarity with the defined knowledge management tools and processes. The results can be displayed in a form such as shown in Figure 5.5, where the score for each tool represents the average level of familiarity (a score of −2 would mean

Figure 5.5 Simple display to show the level of familiarity with the knowledge management toolset across three teams, with positive scores representing high familiarity, and negative scores representing low

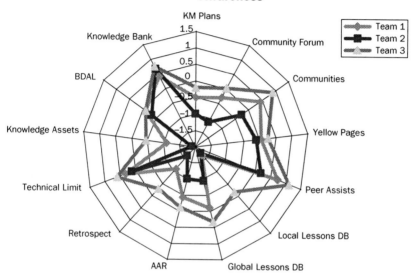

that no team members had never heard of the tool, and a score of +2 would mean they were all experts).

Graphs such as this show that some tools are better deployed than others (in Figure 5.5, peer assists are well understood, but there is much less familiarity with retrospects and knowledge assets), and that some teams are generally more familiar with the toolset than others (Team 3 is more familiar than Team 2).

Effectiveness of knowledge flow within the knowledge management system

The knowledge management framework shown in Figure 5.6 forms an excellent basis for a detailed diagnostic assessment, run at a project, business unit or corporate level, in order to assess the effectiveness of the knowledge management system itself. It therefore differs from the deployment assessments above, as it seeks to measure weaknesses and bottlenecks in the system, rather than how well the system is deployed.

The flow assessment is based on the 12-component Knoco Ltd Framework shown in Figure 1.5, with its four steps of communicating, collecting, organising and accessing, each containing the three enablers of people, process and technology. These four boxes are shown in Figure 5.6 as components of the flow of knowledge from people in one project to people in another. This model provides a theoretical construct to diagnose necessary interventions within the organisation, and enables an identification of the blockages and barriers to the free flow of knowledge within and between projects.

The flow of knowledge through and between the projects has the following components:

- push of knowledge and lessons, from projects with knowledge to offer;
- pull of knowledge and lessons, by projects that need knowledge;
- transfer of tacit knowledge through the 'connect' route, by direct communication;
- transfer of explicit knowledge through the corporate knowledge bank – the 'collect' route – in three steps:
  - collection of the knowledge, or knowledge capture from the projects;

Figure 5.6 A framework for assessing knowledge flow

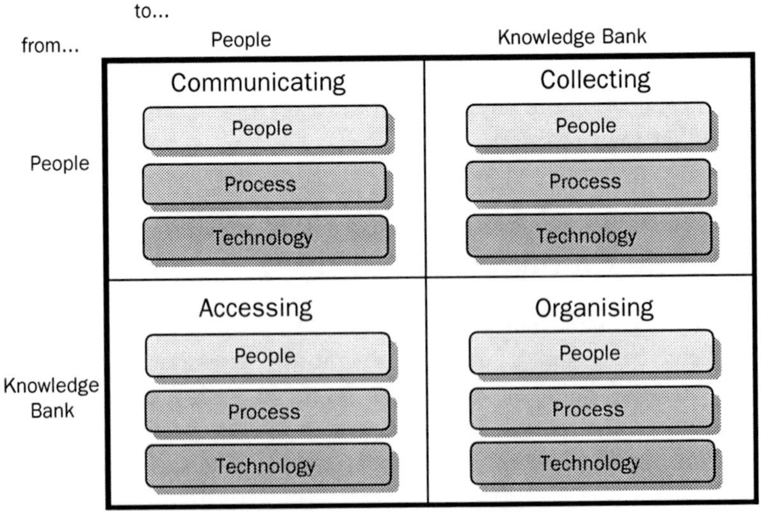

- collation and organisation of the knowledge, and the derivation of best practices and corporate standards;
- accessing the corporate knowledge base by the projects, and publishing and broadcasting new knowledge.

■ each of these steps is facilitated by people (accountable roles and networks), processes, and technology;

■ the flow of knowledge takes place within a corporate culture, which drives the desire, or the reluctance, to push and/or pull knowledge. This culture is set by the leadership elements of the strategic framework shown in Figure 5.1.

Each of the three components of people, process and technology, within the four boxes of communicate, collect, organise and access, is an enabler in the flow of knowledge through a project. Each of these 12 must be functioning properly for knowledge to flow freely. A deficiency in any of these components represents a bottleneck or barrier to the free flow of knowledge. The flow model assessment looks at all these components, gives them a green, yellow or red status (depending on whether the component is fully functioning, is present but needs attention, or is absent), and determines the actions necessary to bring the system up to fit-for-purpose standard.

This sort of assessment should be run at a corporate level, to identify blockages to the free flow of knowledge from one project to another, and

Figure 5.7   **The flow of knowledge from supplier to consumer**

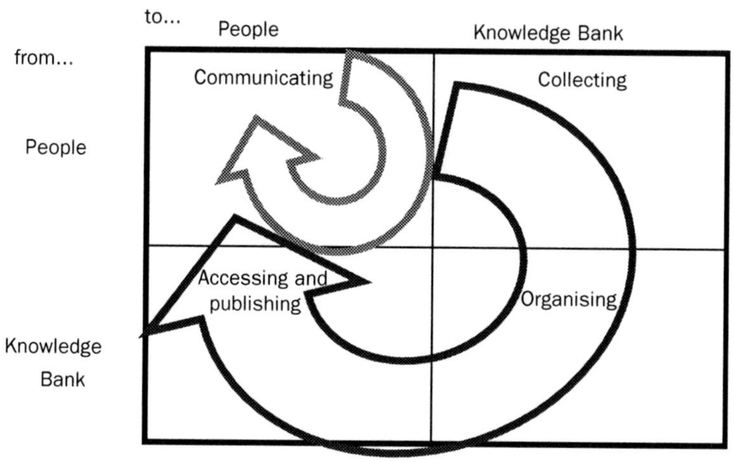

to define potential interventions (new tools, new communities, new standards) to increase knowledge flow.

Assessment of activity level

Even when the knowledge management system is fully operating and fully deployed, there can still be some activity measures put in place.

There are a number of variables that can be measured, including the following:

- Measures of the application of knowledge management in projects, such as the percentage of projects which hold retrospects at each stage, the number of peer assists per project, or the number of lessons coming out of each project. These can be assessed against target levels set by management.

- Measures of the transmission of knowledge between projects, such as the submission of lessons to the corporate lessons database (see Figure 5.8), or the exchange of knowledge in the community discussion forums (see Figure 5.9).

- Measures from the uptake of training (see Figure 5.10), or the use of other corporate knowledge management resources (such as hits on the knowledge management website).

Figure 5.8 Example knowledge management metric, lessons submitted to the lessons database

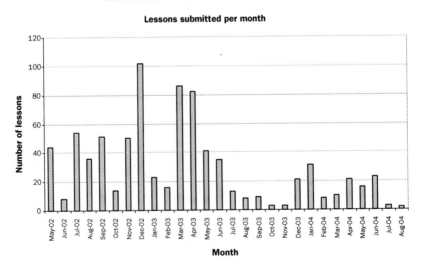

Lessons submitted per month

Figure 5.9 Example knowledge management metric, questions per month in the community discussion forum

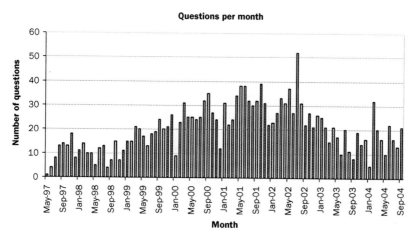

Questions per month

- Measures of the refreshment frequency for knowledge assets, to determine how up-to-date the corporate knowledge store is. These can be assessed against target levels set by management.

The three metrics shown in Figures 5.8–5.10 are real examples from a single company, and all show a decrease in activity in early 2003, linked

Figure 5.10 Example knowledge management metric, take-up of the in-house knowledge management workshop

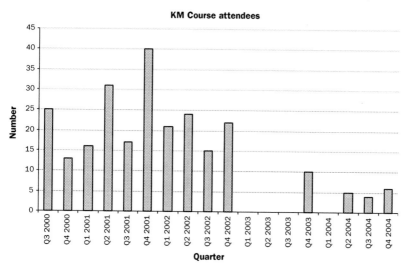

KM Course attendees

to a change in the level of management attention on knowledge management. This has been addressed, with a knowledge management renewal campaign.

Output measurement

If knowledge management is truly deployed in service of performance improvement, then it should impact high-level performance measures such as the cost of projects, the time taken for project delivery, the percentage and level of cost and time over-runs, the level of client satisfaction etc. Although knowledge management is not the sole cause of performance increases, there should be a visible increase in performance as knowledge management is applied.

Interventions and renewal

If the organisation sees worrying signs in any of the measurement methods described above, then interventions can be put in place.

Patchy deployment can be addressed by training programmes, by coaching, and by working with the management teams in areas where knowledge management is not yet deployed. Defects in the system for transferring knowledge within and between projects can be addressed by new or improved tools, new roles or better people in those roles, and new or improved processes. Decreasing activity levels of knowledge exchange within the system can be addressed by renewed leadership focus, renewed engagement and training, clearer accountabilities, or by reviewing the knowledge management strategy (as it is possible that the strategy itself has become outdated).

Support and coordination

The outer elements of the knowledge management strategic framework shown as Figure 5.1 need to be owned and operated by someone, and they generally fall into the remit of a central knowledge management function or team who provide coordination and support.

A central resource

In a large organisation, there may be a need for a small full-time team to own, deliver, monitor and maintain the knowledge management framework. The main responsibilities of this group are:

- To develop, together with the leadership of the organisation, the corporate vision for knowledge management.
- To develop, deliver and maintain the strategy and plan for achieving these objectives.
- To develop, roll out, and update the standards for knowledge management.
- To select, roll out and maintain a systematic approach to knowledge management, including roles, processes, technology.
- To monitor and measure the deployment of this systematic approach, making interventions where required.
- To monitor and measure the effectiveness of this system, making interventions where required.
- To monitor and measure the use of this system, making interventions where required.
- To coordinate and provide knowledge management training to the organisation.
- To coordinate and provide knowledge management reference material to the organisation.
- To work closely with the IT, HR, organisational learning, and communications departments, to ensure that knowledge management complements the other initiatives within the organisation, and provides a common effective infrastructure.

Provision of training

People within the organisation are going to need some training in knowledge management, and the knowledge management framework which will be applied to the projects. Typically there are four levels of training that need to be offered:

- A high-level management overview lasting a few hours, to brief managers in the basic principles, to educate them in what will be expected of them and their teams, and to tell them about the resources and support available to them.

■ A focused workshop for project teams, lasting about one and a half to two days, leading towards the creation of a knowledge management plan. This seeks:

  – to provide project teams with the basic understanding of learning concepts and how to apply them;

  – to provide hands on training in the use of the knowledge management toolbox of processes and technologies;

  – to provide the groundwork for a knowledge management plan.

■ A two-day course for projects professionals (not necessarily all in the same team), for new-recruits, for interested parties in an operational centre, for new areas of operation, and for new alliance or joint-venture partners. This seeks:

  – to provide individuals working in a project teams with the basic understanding of learning concepts and how to apply them;

  – to provide hands on training in the use of the projects toolbox of learning tools and processes.

■ A three-day course for people within the organisation who are playing a specific role in the management of knowledge within the knowledge management framework (for example project knowledge managers, community leaders and subject matter experts). This course seeks:

  – to provide these key individuals who have specific accountabilities for the management of knowledge, with the understanding and skills they need to deliver those accountabilities;

  – to provide hands-on training in the use of the learning tools and processes which will be used within and between the projects;

  – to provide personal experience in knowledge capture and packaging issues.

Provision of reference resources

The organisation will need some knowledge management reference material, so they can look up 'What is a Retrospect', 'How to write a knowledge management plan', etc. The reference material should contain the following:

- a walk-through of the corporate knowledge management strategy and expectations;
- a series of 'how to' guides for the main knowledge management tools and processes;
- a 'knowledge map' for the projects area, listing where the main sources of knowledge are, which communities are available and how to contact them, and who the main subject matter experts and other sources of knowledge are.

Coordinating a knowledge management community of practice

If the organisation is large enough, and there are enough knowledge management activities happening, then it is well worth setting up a knowledge management community of practice. This can be a key enabler of the knowledge management framework and strategy, for the following reasons:

- The knowledge management community will be tremendous advocates for knowledge management within the business, and can greatly facilitate roll-out provided they are given sufficient resources.
- The knowledge management community provides a test-bed for knowledge management tools and techniques.
- The knowledge management community of practice will be heavily involved in sustaining knowledge management in the organisation, once the initial roll-out of the framework is over.
- The community members are a great support for each other, both in practical terms (exchanging good practices in knowledge management) and in terms of solidarity and emotional support.

Coordination of the knowledge management community is one of the roles of the central knowledge management team.

6

The linkage with other management disciplines

Knowledge management needs to be closely linked with the other disciplines within the project, as an important component of the entire project management framework. Some of the key interactions are listed below.

Performance management

The knowledge/performance loop shown in Figure 6.1 (a copy of Figure 1.7) shows the close link between knowledge and performance, and it is fairly obvious from this link that knowledge management and performance management are also strongly linked. The management systems can be linked in the following ways:

- The frequency of lessons capture should be linked with the frequency of performance measurement. Knowledge capture exercises such as retrospects and after action reviews (Chapter 3) are based on an analysis of 'what actually happened' compared with 'what was expected to happen', i.e. an analysis of actual performance versus target performance. Therefore, every time performance is measured and compared with target performance, there is an opportunity to capture lessons. So, for example, if performance is reported at monthly project meetings, then an after action review can be built into the meeting to capture the lessons that arise (see Chapter 3).

- Underperformance should be seen as a learning opportunity. For example, when any BP major project over-runs its budget sufficiently to require sanction of additional funds, a special learning exercise is

Figure 6.1 The knowledge/performance loop

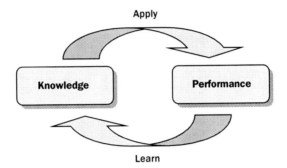

commissioned by the head of projects, in order to draw out the learning for future projects.

Risk management

Knowledge management and risk management are also closely linked. Both are disciplines for managing the intangible factors that affect the operation of a project. Both need to be managed through the life of a project. Risk management and knowledge management also interact in the following ways:

- The project team may need to learn what risks the project is facing. Other projects may be able to identify risks of which the project team was otherwise unaware. An analysis of lessons from past projects can also identify the common risks that need to be managed.

- Acquisition of knowledge is a way to reduce risk, or to manage risk. Risks can be mitigated if you know what to do. Risks can also be avoided, if you know how to avoid them. Many of the areas of project risk identified in the risk management exercise, are areas where knowledge needs to be acquired, and should therefore appear in the knowledge management plan. There should be significant correlation and coordination between the risk management plan and the knowledge management plan.

- There will probably be significant overlap between the knowledge register (Chapter 5) and the risk register. It might even be worth considering combining the two registers.

SSHE management

Safety, security, health and the environment (SSHE) are key areas of focus for many project operations. Good performance in these areas is not only a social duty; it also is a component of maintaining your licence to operate. However, these may be very difficult areas to manage, particularly when working with a number of sub-contractors with varying interpretation of SSHE expectations, or in developing countries where SSHE performance has not been an area of focus, or where security may be an issue.

Knowledge management interacts with SSHE management in two main ways.

■ Knowledge management can be a way of ensuring the project learns about the SSHE risks, and how to avoid them. In areas where this is an issue, SSHE should be identified as a key knowledge area in the project knowledge management plan. The person accountable for this area of knowledge can then look for past projects with valuable experience, can set up processes to bring this knowledge into the project, and can join any SSHE communities of practice which can provide useful guidance. This level of proactive knowledge management is crucial, if the project hopes to minimise or avoid accidents, illnesses, security breaches or environmental breaches.

■ Knowledge management can help the project (and the organisation) to learn from any incidents that might occur during project planning and execution. A learning system from incidents needs to be set up, involving root cause analysis, the derivation of lessons (for sharing) and actions (for addressing any identified issues), for tracking the actions and for sharing the lessons.

7

Summary

This book has been a detailed walk-though of knowledge management as it applies to teams and projects, and the reader may be feeling a little overwhelmed by it all! This final chapter seeks to summarise the main conclusions for three groups of key knowledge management users: the project managers and knowledge managers, the community coordinators and SMEs, and the company management.

For the project manager, and project knowledge manager

- The project manager needs to ensure that the project staff are learning before doing.
- Scoping meetings are a way of bringing knowledge during the scoping phase of the project.
- Customer interview maximises the team's knowledge of the customers' needs and context.
- The earlier you can bring in contractors' knowledge, the better.
- Peer assist is one of the simplest and most effective ways of bringing in existing knowledge from past projects.
- Optioneering is one form of peer assist.
- If there is no existing knowledge, some level of business-driven action learning may be needed.
- Peer review is more of an assurance process than a knowledge management process.
- Technical limit is an excellent process for accessing the knowledge of the execution team prior to execution.

- The project manager needs to ensure that the project staff are 'learning while doing.'

- The after action review is an excellent way of doing this.

- Communities of practice are a crucial resource for learning while doing.

- After action reviews can be built into project review meetings.

- The project manager will need to appoint a knowledge manager for the project.

- Knowledge engineers and/or learning historians may also be needed in major projects.

- A lessons and action log will be needed.

- The project manager needs to ensure that the project staff are learning after doing.

- Retrospects need to be scheduled after each project stage (and perhaps more frequently).

- On a large or dispersed project, a knowledge history may be needed.

- Knowledge management needs to be linked with performance management, risk management, and SSHE management.

For the community coordinators and SMEs

- Ownership needs to be established for the management of knowledge between the projects, and for the derivation of best practices and standards.

- A lessons learned database may be needed for the projects.

- Best practices, knowledge assets and corporate standards should be constructed for key areas of knowledge.

- Subject matter experts are needed for these key knowledge areas.

- Transfer of tacit knowledge can be facilitated through staff transfer and communities of practice.

- A Yellow Pages system is also a useful tool.

For management

- The organisation needs a knowledge management framework.
- Knowledge management standards need to be developed.
- Knowledge management plans should be introduced at project level.
- Some sort of audit or assessment of knowledge management capability is needed.
- A resource is needed for monitoring, support, and coordination of knowledge management activities (including performance measurement and the provision of training).

Bibliography

Collison, C. and Parcell, G. (2004) *Learning to Fly: Practical Knowledge Management from Leading and Learning Organisations.* Oxford: Capstone Press.

Davenport, T. H. and Prusak, L. (2000) *Working Knowledge.* Boston, MA: Harvard Business School Press.

Dixon, N. M. (2000) *Common Knowledge: How Companies Thrive by Sharing What They Know.* Boston, MA: Harvard Business School Press.

Dolan, S. P., Williams, G. J., Barrows, W. J., Dickson, J. W., Torry, D. and Drury, R. F. (2003) 'Performance Improvement Techniques Used on a Goodwyn A Platform, North-west Shelf, Australia'. *SPE Drilling and Completions Journal*, 18(2): 138–145.

Gorelick, C., April, K. and Milton, N. (2004) *Performance Through Learning: Knowledge Management in Practice.* Burlington, MA: Butterworth-Heinemann.

Nonaka, I., Takeuchi, H. (1995) *The Knowledge-Creating Company: How Japanese Companies Create the Dynamics of Innovation.* Oxford: Oxford University Press.

Rumizen, M. C. (2001) *The Complete Idiot's Guide to Knowledge Management.* New York: Penguin Putnam.

Wenger, E., McDermott, R., Snyder W. M. (2002) *Cultivating Communities of Practice.* Boston, MA: Harvard Business School Press.

Index

Knowledge Management for Teams and Projects

Lightning Source UK Ltd.
Milton Keynes UK
UKOW042240280613

212927UK00001B/20/A